GOOD
HOUSEKEEPING

The Best-Ever Cookie Book

GOOD
HOUSEKEEPING

The Best-Ever
Cookie Book

175 TESTED-'TIL-PERFECT RECIPES
FOR CRISPY, CHEWY & OOEY-GOOEY TREATS

Edited By Tiffany Blackstone,
Trish Clasen & Kate Merker

FOREWORD BY
Jane Francisco

HEARST
HOME

Contents

Frosted Lemon Ricotta Cookies

Salted Chocolate Caramel Cookies

Chinese Almond Cookies

Blueberry Crumb Bars

Foreword

One of my favorite things about working at *Good Housekeeping* is popping upstairs to the Test Kitchen for a meeting only to be greeted with a fresh-from-the-oven cookie.

Whether it's a buttery shortbread square layered with fudgy ganache or a chewy chocolate chip cookie so tasty you would never guess it's vegan, I know it's going to be good. That's because our Test Kitchen team bakes around a thousand cookies every year.

Every one of our editors and culinary pros has discovered a tried-and-true favorite (mine: Chewy Chocolate-Walnut Cookies, page 64). Our chief food director, Kate Merker, keeps a batch of Oatmeal Chocolate Chip dough (page 36) in the Test Kitchen freezer for when a craving strikes! So when the idea came about to fill a cookbook with our best-ever cookie recipes, it was an easy decision. Why wouldn't we want to share?!

Inside, you'll find a collection of the best cookies to come out of our Test Kitchen ovens — including our Blueberry Crumb Bars (page 122), Oatmeal Cream Pies (page 154) and Red Velvet Snowballs (page 80), to name a few. Ready to find a new favorite? Here's what you need to know:

- We organized these recipes by baking method — drop cookies, slice and bakes, bars and other creations — so you can choose a cookie based on your mood and how much time you have.

- There's one exception: The final chapter in this book is filled with fun, festive recipes for all

sorts of celebrations. Whether you're looking for a sweet treat to make for Valentine's Day, Lunar New Year, Easter, Passover or Halloween, there's something here for you.

- You'll learn how to transform a batch of sugar cookie cutouts into something gorgeous with tricks from the pros. (Fun fact: Our Test Kitchen team goes through 30-plus pounds of confectioners' sugar each year to make Royal Icing for Christmas and Easter cookies alone!)

- We've filled this book with beautiful ways to package up these sweets. Peep the "Gift It!" tips for the prettiest presentation ideas.

- Our bonus gift: a cookie countdown calendar for December with 25 deliciously different ways to decorate a batch of sugar cookies (page 242).

We hope these treats sweeten up your day, whether it's a birthday, special occasion or any given Wednesday. Happy baking!

Jane

Jane Francisco
Editor-in-Chief

Vegan
Chocolate
Chip
Cookies

35

Chapter 1

Bake Your Best Cookies

Get the (baked) goods on setting up your kitchen, measuring and decorating — plus clever shortcuts, pretty packaging ideas and more. The only things you need to bring are an appetite and a frosty glass of milk.

JAMMIN' HEART COOKIES 193

←

Cookie Baking Basics

These Test Kitchen tricks will help you take your baked goods to the next level — whether you're a rookie or a cookie-making pro.

When baking, always...

- Read the recipe from beginning to end before starting. Seriously!

- Gather all the ingredients, equipment and tools you will need (a.k.a. mise en place).

- Place the oven racks in the correct positions before turning on the oven. Most of the recipes in this book use the center oven rack.

- Heat the oven at least 15 minutes before you put anything in it. Always, always, always wait for the oven to come to temperature before you start baking.

- Set the timer once your project is in the oven. Pro tip: Subtract one minute from the timer so you have time to make sure you're ready (potholders, toothpicks, etc.).

- Keep clean, dry oven mitts or pads nearby and get your cooling racks set up as soon as your cookies go into the oven.

- Mix dough only until blended after adding the flour, unless the recipe says otherwise. Overmixing results in tough cookies.

- Add oats or chocolate chips to your dry ingredients before mixing with wet ingredients to ensure those bits of goodness are evenly distributed throughout your batch.

- Bake cookies one sheet at a time in the center of the oven. In a time crunch, you can put one sheet in the lower third of the oven, one in the top third, and rotate the sheets (top to bottom and front to back) halfway through the baking time.

- Let baking sheets cool between batches. You should never place cookie dough on a hot baking sheet; the heat will melt the dough before it has had a chance to set, resulting in cookies that are too flat.

- Pack cooled cookies in an airtight container with parchment paper between each layer for perfect freezing; freeze for up to 3 months.

Equip Your Kitchen

Make sure your kitchen is stocked with the right tools to set yourself up for (delicious) success.

Baking Pans

When making bars, blondies and brownies, it's important to match the size of the pan to whatever the recipe calls for (yes, it really matters!). Check the bottom of the pan for measurements or use a ruler to measure the top of the dish from inside edge to inside edge.

Cookie Cutters

Choose shapes you'll use often and get creative.

Baking Sheets

Heavy-gauge aluminum is great. Your baking sheets should be at least 2 inches smaller in length and width than your oven so that the hot air can circulate freely around the sheets.

Cookie Scoops

They are key to measuring out equal portions of dough that will bake in the same amount of time, ensuring all of your cookies are evenly baked.

Electric Mixer

Either a stand mixer or hand mixer will work to cream butter, combine batter and make the fluffiest whipped cream. But a stand mixer will come in clutch for anything requiring you to mix for a longer period of time. (Hello, meringues!)

Measuring Cups

You'll need two types: a nested set of metal or plastic scoops to measure dry ingredients, and clear glass or plastic cups with pouring spouts to measure liquids.

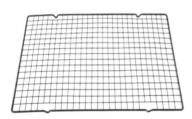

Cooling Racks

Large rectangular wire racks allow air to circulate around cookies after they are removed from the oven. (Cookies will continue to bake if left on the hot baking sheets!)

Food Processor

From chopping nuts to making a graham cracker crumb crust, this kitchen appliance can shave minutes off the prep time.

Measuring Spoons

Baking is a science, so be sure to measure everything correctly. For more about proper measuring, see Measuring 101 (page 16).

Rolling Pin

The classic rolling pin spins between two handles. Some bakers prefer a longer dowel-style pin. This straight cylinder style is sometimes called a Shaker rolling pin; one with tapered ends is called a French pin.

Mixing Bowls

Keep a few on hand, since it's typically best to mix dry ingredients and wet ingredients separately before combining. Plus, it's a drag to have to stop in the middle of a recipe to wash out a bowl.

Offset Spatula

This long, narrow spatula is ideal for spreading frosting onto cookies or loosening the edges of brownies, blondies and bars from the pan.

Parchment Paper

Whether it's lining a baking sheet or baking pan (with overhang), parchment paper makes it easier to remove cookies. The result: No mess, no stress.

Piping Bag

Paired with decorating tips, this is used to pipe icing or frosting onto cookies. Use a coupler if you intend to swap decorating tips without changing out piping bags.

Resealable Plastic Bags

Use them as backup piping bags (just add frosting, seal and snip off one corner) or to store batter or dough before baking.

Silicone Baking Mats

For an environmentally friendly way to line baking sheets, try these reusable mats instead of using parchment paper.

Small Cookie Spatula

For flawless removal, use this type of spatula to transfer cookies from baking sheets to cooling racks. Other spatulas (fish spatulas, pancake turners) can also get the job done.

Spatulas

Heatproof silicone spatulas are a favorite for baking because you don't need to worry about them warping in a hot pan when making caramel or chocolate sauce.

Toothpicks

Use them to add pulled frosting details to cookies. Drag a toothpick through frosting or icing while it's still wet to create a pretty visual effect.

Tweezers

Invest in a new pair to use only in the kitchen. They're great for placing decorative details, like sprinkles and small candies, onto cookies.

Measuring 101

When it comes to baking, recipes depend on the correct ratio of ingredients — plus chemistry — to work. Unlike soups and stews, where too much or too little of an ingredient blends in without much consequence, what you add to — or subtract from — a cookie recipe could affect the final texture.

Follow these steps to ensure precise measuring while baking:

For liquids, use a clear measuring cup with a spout. Place it on a flat surface and add the desired amount of liquid. Bend down to check the accuracy; don't try to gauge from above.

For dry ingredients, spoon and sweep the ingredient into flat-topped measuring cups. When measuring flour, stir it with a fork or whisk to aerate it before spooning (it tends to settle and pack down during storage). Overfill the cup slightly and then use a straightedge or metal spatula to level it off. Don't scoop the cup directly into flour; you'll pack it down, and the result will be a drier baked good.

Brown sugar, butter and shortening — unlike flour — should be firmly packed into the cup and hold its shape when turned out.

When measuring sticky ingredients like molasses, honey or syrup, lightly grease the cup with vegetable oil or cooking spray first. The ingredient will slide out, leaving none behind.

Equivalent Measurements

This convenient chart will help you measure with accuracy.

Pinch = amount you can pick up between your thumb and forefinger (about ¼ teaspoon)

Dash = less than ⅛ teaspoon

 1 tablespoon = 3 teaspoons   **1 pound** = 16 ounces

½ tablespoon = 1½ teaspoons   **¾ pound** = 12 ounces

 1 cup = ½ pint   **½ pound** = 8 ounces

2 cups = 1 pint   **¼ pound** = 4 ounces

4 cups
= 1 quart

Tablespoon Measurements

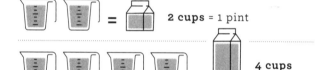

4 tablespoons = ¼ cup

5 tablespoons plus 1 teaspoon = ⅓ cup

 **10 tablespoons plus 2 teaspoons** = ⅔ cup

8 tablespoons = ½ cup

12 tablespoons = ¾ cup

16 tablespoons = 1 cup

Basic Cookie Doughs

With simple additions — sprinkles, icing, candies and more! — you can transform these three basic doughs into treats for any occasion. Need some ideas? Turn to Chapter 6 (page 186) for inspiration.

Classic Sugar Cookie Dough

Active Time 10 minutes
Total Time 25 minutes, plus chilling and cooling
Makes 36 to 48 (depending on size and shape)

2 ¾   cups all-purpose flour

½   teaspoon baking powder

½   teaspoon kosher salt

1   cup (2 sticks) unsalted butter, at room temperature

¾   cup granulated sugar

1   large egg

1 ½   teaspoons pure vanilla extract

1. In a large bowl, whisk together flour, baking powder and salt; set aside.

2. Using an electric mixer, beat butter and sugar in another large bowl on medium speed until light and fluffy, 3 minutes.

Beat in egg and then vanilla. Reduce speed to low and gradually add flour mixture, mixing until just incorporated.

3. Shape dough into 3 disks and roll each between 2 sheets of parchment paper to ⅛ to ¼ inch thick. Chill until firm, 30 minutes in the refrigerator or 15 minutes in the freezer.

4. Heat oven to 350°F. Line 2 baking sheets with parchment paper. Using floured cookie cutters, cut out cookies and place them onto the prepared sheets, spacing them 2 inches apart. Reroll, chill and cut the scraps.

5. Bake, rotating the positions of the baking sheets halfway through, until cookies are light golden brown around edges, 10 to 12 minutes. Let cool on baking sheets for 5 minutes before transferring to a cooling rack to cool completely.

PER SERVING
About 85 calories, 5 g fat (3 g saturated fat), 1 g protein, 30 mg sodium, 10 g carbohydrates, 0 g fiber

Spiced Cookie Dough

Active Time 10 minutes | **Total Time** 25 minutes, plus chilling and cooling
Makes 36 to 48 (depending on size and shape)

3	cups all-purpose flour
½	teaspoon ground cinnamon
½	teaspoon ground ginger
¼	teaspoon ground cloves
¾	teaspoon baking powder
½	teaspoon kosher salt
1	cup (2 sticks) unsalted butter, at room temperature
1	cup granulated sugar
1	large egg
2	tablespoons molasses
2	teaspoons pure vanilla extract
1	teaspoon pure almond extract

1. In a large bowl, whisk together flour, cinnamon, ginger, cloves, baking powder and salt; set aside.

2. Using an electric mixer, beat butter and sugar in another large bowl on medium-high speed until light and fluffy, 3 minutes. Beat in egg, then molasses and extracts until combined.

3. Reduce speed to low and gradually add flour mixture, mixing until just incorporated.

4. Shape dough into 3 disks and roll each between 2 sheets of parchment paper to ⅛ to ¼ inch thick. Chill until firm, 30 minutes in the refrigerator or 15 minutes in the freezer.

5. Heat oven to 375°F. Line 2 baking sheets with parchment paper. Using floured cookie cutters, cut out cookies and place them onto the prepared sheets, spacing them 2 inches apart. Reroll, chill and cut the scraps.

6. Bake, rotating the positions of the baking sheets halfway through, until cookies are light golden brown around edges, 10 to 12 minutes. Let cool on baking sheets for 5 minutes before transferring to a cooling rack to cool completely.

PER SERVING
About 95 calories, 5 g fat (3 g saturated fat), 1 g protein, 35 mg sodium, 13 g carbohydrates, 0 g fiber

Shaping (and Rolling!) Smarts

Rolling out sugar cookie dough can be tricky. If you roll out the dough without chilling it first, it sticks to your counter. But if you chill it first to make it less sticky, it's as hard as a rock. Try this: Roll out dough between 2 sheets of parchment paper before chilling it. That way the dough won't cling to your rolling pin (or countertop). Pop the whole thing into the fridge for 30 minutes to chill. Then cut out your cookie shapes mess-free.

Black Cocoa Cookie Dough

Active Time 10 minutes | **Total Time** 55 minutes
Makes 36 to 48 (depending on size and shape)

2	cups all-purpose flour
¼	cup unsweetened cocoa
¼	cup unsweetened black cocoa
½	teaspoon baking soda
¼	teaspoon kosher salt
¾	cup (1 ½ sticks) unsalted butter, at room temperature
¾	cup granulated sugar
1	large egg
2	teaspoons pure vanilla extract

1. In a medium bowl, whisk together flour, cocoas, baking soda and salt; set aside.

2. Using an electric mixer, beat butter and sugar in a large bowl on medium-high speed until fluffy, about 3 minutes. Beat in egg, then vanilla. Reduce speed to low and gradually add flour mixture, mixing until incorporated.

3. Shape dough into 2 disks and roll each between 2 sheets of parchment paper to ⅛ to ¼ inch thick. Chill until firm, 30 minutes in the refrigerator or 15 minutes in the freezer.

4. Heat oven to 350°F. Line 2 baking sheets with parchment paper. Using cocoa-dusted cutters, cut out cookies. Place onto the prepared sheets, spacing them 2 inches apart. Reroll, chill and cut the scraps.

5. Bake, rotating the positions of the baking sheets halfway through, until cookies are light golden brown around edges, 10 to 12 minutes. Let cool on baking sheets for 5 minutes before transferring to a cooling rack to cool completely.

PER SERVING
About 80 calories, 4 g fat (2.5 g saturated fat), 1 g protein, 35 mg sodium, 10 g carbohydrates, 0 g fiber

Shortcut Sugar Cookie Cutouts

Skip straight to the rolling and shaping with this easy hack that turns slice-and-bake dough into holiday cutout cookies in seconds.

1   **16.5-ounce package refrigerated ready-made sugar cookie dough**

½   **cup all-purpose flour, plus more for surfaces**

1. ADD FLOUR

Break dough into pieces. On a well-floured surface, knead dough until soft. Knead flour into dough, a little bit at a time, until just incorporated.

2. ROLL AND CUT

Form dough into a disk. Lightly flour the rolling pin and your surface, then roll dough to ¼ inch thick. Using floured cookie cutters, cut out cookies. Reroll and repeat with remaining dough.

3. DRESS 'EM UP

Transfer cutouts to a parchment-lined baking sheet, spacing them 2 inches apart. For the easiest decorating ever, sprinkle them with colored sanding sugars.

4. CHILL, THEN BAKE

Freeze cookies on the prepared sheet for at least 30 minutes to help maintain their shape, then bake as the package directs.

Decorating 101

With these recipes — and a complete step-by-step guide to icing and flooding (page 26) — you'll be confidently decorating cookies in no time at all.

Royal Icing

This icing is ideal for adding intricate details and designs, and it hardens to a candy-like shell.

Active Time 5 minutes | **Total Time** 12 minutes | **Makes** 2 to 4 cups

3 large egg whites

½ teaspoon cream of tartar

16 ounces confectioners' sugar

Gel food coloring, optional

TEST KITCHEN TIP

Because this icing contains uncooked egg whites, it may be best for children, pregnant women, the elderly and those with compromised immune systems to avoid eating it. Instead, use Decorator's Icing (at right).

1. Using an electric mixer, whisk egg whites and cream of tartar in a large bowl on medium-high speed until foamy, about 1 minute.

2. Reduce speed to low and gradually add sugar, beating until just incorporated. Increase speed to high and beat until medium-stiff glossy peaks form, 5 to 7 minutes.

3. To add color: Separate icing into bowls and tint different colors with gel food coloring, then transfer to separate piping bags fitted with fine tips.

PER SERVING

About 40 calories, 0 g fat (0 g saturated fat), 0 g protein, 5 mg sodium, 10 g carbohydrates, 0 g fiber

Decorator's Icing

Similar to Royal Icing, this icing is made with meringue powder — a baking substitute made from dried egg whites — instead of raw eggs.

Active Time 5 minutes | **Total Time** 10 minutes
Makes 3 cups

- 16 ounces confectioners' sugar
- 3 tablespoons meringue powder
- ⅓ cup warm water
- Gel food coloring, optional

1. Using an electric mixer, beat confectioners' sugar, meringue powder and warm water in a large bowl on medium speed until blended and mixture is very stiff, about 5 minutes.

2. Tint icing with food coloring as desired; press plastic wrap directly onto surface to prevent it from drying out.

3. When ready to decorate, use a small spatula or piping bags fitted with small writing tips to ice cookies.

PER SERVING
About 40 calories, 0 g fat (0 g saturated fat), 0 g protein, 5 mg sodium, 10 g carbohydrates, 0 g fiber

Vanilla Buttercream

Rich and creamy, this frosting does not dry hard like icing, so keep this in mind when storing (do not stack!).

Active Time 5 minutes | **Total Time** 10 minutes
Makes 3 cups

- 16 ounces confectioners' sugar
- 1 cup (2 sticks) unsalted butter, at room temperature
- 1 to 2 tablespoons heavy cream
- 2 teaspoons pure vanilla extract
- ¼ teaspoon kosher salt
- Gel food coloring, optional

1. Sift confectioners' sugar into a bowl.

2. Using an electric mixer, beat butter in a large bowl on medium speed until creamy, about 2 minutes.

3. Reduce speed to low and gradually add sugar, alternating with heavy cream. Mix in vanilla and salt. Increase speed to high and beat until fluffy, about 2 minutes. Divide and tint as desired.

PER SERVING
About 75 calories, 4 g fat (3 g saturated fat), 0 g protein, 10 mg sodium, 10 g carbohydrates, 0 g fiber

Switch It Up!
Chocolate Buttercream
Prepare Vanilla Buttercream, mixing in **14 ounces melted and cooled bittersweet chocolate** along with the vanilla extract. Omit food coloring.

1. OUTLINE

With slow, steady pressure, use the thicker icing and a fine tip to outline the cookie (or the area) you want to color. Let the outline dry.

Flood Like a Pro

Mix up a batch of Royal Icing or Decorator's Icing (pages 24 and 25), and tint as desired with paste or gel food coloring. Thin out half with a few drops of water until it's the consistency of honey, then pop the thick and thin icings into two separate piping bags. Now let's get decorating!

2. FILL

Cut a ½-inch opening from the piping bag with the thinned icing. Squeeze some icing into the outlined area and use a toothpick to drag it to the outlined edge — this is called flooding.

3. SPRINKLE

Add colored sugar crystals or other decorations while the icing is wet. Or let dry and then pipe a design in a contrasting color on top.

Your Ultimate Cookie Gifting & Sharing Guide

Fact: Cookies taste even better when they're enjoyed with others! Here's how to spread the love.

How to Host a Cookie Swap

Similar to a potluck, each guest comes to the party with a dish in hand — but instead of casseroles, your home will be overflowing with cookies!

1. Invite four to eight friends, each with a unique cookie to share. Keep track of who is bringing what, so no one doubles up. You'll want to make sure there is enough variety too, in terms of flavor profiles and types of cookies.

2. Ask everyone to bake a dozen cookies per guest, plus extras for tasting. Don't forget copies of the recipes!

3. Set a table with empty platters labeled with the bakers' names and cookie descriptions. Have each guest display their cookies on their assigned platter and stack recipe cards nearby.

4. Serve hot chocolate or coffee for dunking. Have savory snacks on hand too, to offset the sweetness.

5. Provide packing supplies — including parchment paper to separate layers of cookies — for takeaways or remind friends to bring containers.

Genius Ways to Gift Goodies

- Stock up on plain cookie tins whenever they're on sale, or get some from the local craft or dollar store. Upgrade tins with pretty ribbon and colorful tissue paper before filling with cookies.

- Line a mini loaf pan with tissue paper and waxed paper. Add cookies, wrap with cellophane, secure with a ribbon and attach a recipe card with a handwritten note.

- To gift one cookie (e.g., a delicately decorated sugar cookie), place it in a cardboard jewelry gift box.

- Mason jars can be used for so much more than preserving jams. These versatile glass containers make beautiful vessels for gifting cookies. All you need is ribbon to dress it up. Feeling extra? Glue some scent-sational cinnamon sticks to the lid!

- Line a shirt box with tissue paper. Cut parchment paper into small squares and layer between cookies.

- Wrap the edges of a cardboard pie slice box with decorative ribbon. Wrap cookies in parchment, then secure with a ribbon and tuck inside the box.

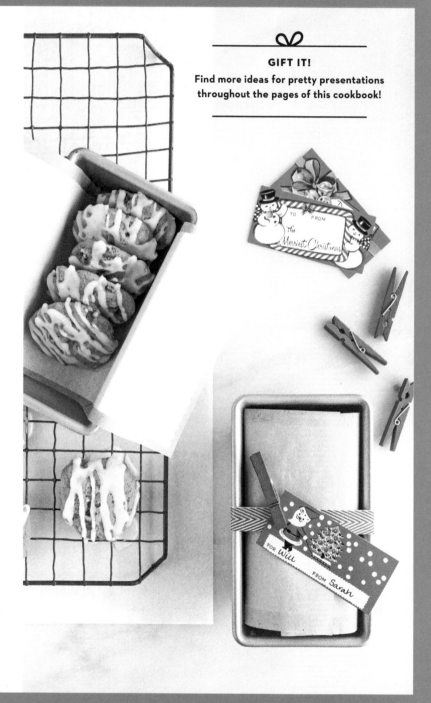

GIFT IT!
Find more ideas for pretty presentations throughout the pages of this cookbook!

Bake Sale Basics

You don't need to be a member of the PTA to appreciate a grade-A cookie, bar or cupcake. Here's how to add more flavor to a fundraiser:

- Check in with your town hall or school about health rules and permits before you start planning.

- The more (help) the merrier! Create a bake sale committee, enlist friends and divvy up tasks.

- Reach out to the pros: Bakeries and restaurants might be happy to contribute if you display their business cards.

- Label *everything*, from names and prices to any potential allergens. Include a list of ingredients too, for anyone with dietary restrictions. Cardstock tags from a paper store or Etsy make for great labels, or create your own by cutting up old greeting cards and gift bags.

- Be strategic with your serveware: Raid your cabinets or the local dollar store for plates and trays in various sizes and colors. Create multiple levels to display more treats (cake stands come in handy here!). Group wrapped items and divide among platters.

- Make sure everyone knows about your bake sale and what you're raising money for! Craft signs, banners and labels, and use social media to help spread the word.

Party Favor Picks

Any festivity is sweeter when guests can easily grab a cookie.

- Stock up on festive takeout boxes and pretty tissue paper. Line each box with tissue paper and top with sugary treats.

- Place one cookie in a cellophane bag for each guest. Fold the top and secure it with a "Hello, my name is..." sticker. Label each with a guest's name and seating assignment (if applicable). Using clothespins and a line of jute, hang the bags so guests can find their names!

- Set out an assortment of cookies, plus a stack of glassine envelopes and stickers, with a note for guests to take a favorite to go.

Mailing Cookies 101

Ship your cookies with care, following these instructions so they won't crumble:

- Avoid delicate cookies. In *GH*'s tests, sturdy cookies (think thick sugar stars or biscotti) survived shipping; tuiles didn't.

- Pack 'em tight. Use waxed paper to line tins and separate layers. Fill empty spaces with crumpled waxed paper.

- Bubble-wrap the tin. Use enough to keep it snug in the shipping box. This reduces the risk of cookies breaking in transit.

Chapter 2

Drop Cookies

There's a reason some of the most popular cookie recipes fall into this category (hello, chocolate chip!): Spoonfuls of soft dough transform into melt-in-your-mouth cookies with practically no effort. Plus, the flavor combinations are endless.

CHEWY CHOCOLATE–WALNUT COOKIES 64

←

Chocolate Chip Cookies

Perhaps the most popular cookie out there, these sweets are filled with bits of melty chocolate. Plus, we figured out how to make them vegan (and delicious all the same!).

Chewy Chocolate Chip Cookies

Active Time 25 minutes
Total Time 45 minutes, plus chilling
Makes 16

3 ⅓	cups all-purpose flour
⅓	cup cornstarch
1½	teaspoons baking powder
1¼	teaspoons baking soda
1¼	teaspoons kosher salt
1¼	cups (2 ½ sticks) unsalted butter, at room temperature
1½	cups firmly packed dark brown sugar
¾	cup granulated sugar
2	large eggs
1	tablespoon pure vanilla extract
1	pound bittersweet chocolate chunks
2	cups walnuts or pecans, toasted (optional)

1. In a large bowl, combine flour, cornstarch, baking powder and baking soda; set aside.

2. Using an electric mixer, beat butter and sugars in a large bowl on medium speed until very light and fluffy, about 5 minutes. Add eggs, one at a time, mixing well after each addition. Stir in vanilla. Reduce speed to low, add dry ingredients and mix until just combined, 5 to 10 seconds. Fold in chocolate and walnuts, if using. Transfer dough to a large resealable plastic bag and refrigerate for at least 24 hours and up to 72 hours.

3. Heat oven to 350°F. Line a baking sheet with parchment paper.

4. Scoop 6 scant ½ cupfuls of chilled dough onto the prepared sheet, spacing them 3 inches apart. Bake until golden brown at edges but still very soft in center (cookies will look very underbaked), 18 (for chewy) to 20 minutes. Transfer the baking sheet to a cooling rack. For crisper edges, transfer cookies from the sheet to cool on a cooling rack. For the chewiest cookies, let cool completely on the baking sheet. Repeat or store remaining dough.

PER SERVING
About 500 calories, 27 g fat (16 g saturated fat), 7 g protein, 350 mg sodium, 66 g carbohydrates, 4 g fiber

Vegan Chocolate Chip Cookies

Active Time 20 minutes
Total Time 35 minutes, plus freezing
Makes 24

2	cups all-purpose flour
1	teaspoon baking soda
½	teaspoon kosher salt
1	cup dairy-free bittersweet chocolate chips
1	cup dairy-free semisweet chocolate chips
½	cup firmly packed dark brown sugar
½	cup granulated sugar
½	cup canola oil
¼	cup water
2	teaspoons pure vanilla extract

1. In a medium bowl, whisk together flour, baking soda and salt. Toss with chocolate chips; set aside.

2. In a second bowl, break up brown sugar, making sure there are no lumps. Add granulated sugar, oil, water and vanilla, and whisk to combine. Add flour mixture and mix until just combined (there should be no streaks of flour).

3. Line 2 baking sheets with parchment paper. Scoop ¼ cupfuls of dough onto the prepared sheets, spacing them 2 inches apart, gently gathering dough together with hands without pressing. (Dough will be crumbly.) Freeze for 30 minutes.

4. Heat oven to 375°F. Bake, rotating the positions of the baking sheets after 6 minutes, until edges are golden brown, 10 to 13 minutes total (cookies will be soft and will continue to cook). Let cool on baking sheets on a cooling rack.

PER SERVING
About 400 calories, 20.5 g fat (7 g saturated fat),
4 g protein, 190 mg sodium, 50 g carbohydrates, 1 g fiber

Your Chocolate Chip Cookie Cheat Sheet

These tricks and tips from the Test Kitchen will help you achieve the results you're looking for.

BRING BUTTER (AND EGGS) TO ROOM TEMPERATURE

Softened butter (and eggs at room temperature) will beat fluffier, incorporate sugar more easily and make your flour easier to fold in.

CHOOSE THE RIGHT SIZE COOKIE

There's a reason those chewy cookies are often so big. Using between 4 and 6 ounces of dough per cookie makes it possible for the edges to crisp and the centers to remain soft and chewy. Want crisper cookies? Make them smaller.

SLIGHTLY UNDERBAKE COOKIES, THEN COOL ON THE PAN

While this is usually a no-no because it can steam baked goods, it is actually the perfect way to keep your cookies chewy. (Note: You must bake them for less time for this to work properly.) If you like a crisp cookie, remove from the pan after a few minutes as noted.

FOR VEGAN COOKIES, SUB IN CANOLA OIL

This is the secret to creating ooey-gooey chocolate chip cookies so good, no one will ever guess there are no eggs or butter.

Oatmeal Chocolate Chip Cookies

Chocolate chips replace raisins for a take on the classic oatmeal cookie. These are great for cinnamon lovers, but drop the cinnamon to ½ teaspoon if you're looking for a more subtle flavor.

Active Time 30 minutes | **Total Time** 1 hour 15 minutes | **Makes** 20

1½	cups all-purpose flour
1	teaspoon ground cinnamon
1	teaspoon baking soda
½	teaspoon kosher salt
¼	teaspoon freshly grated nutmeg
2	cups old-fashioned rolled oats
2	cups dairy-free bittersweet chocolate chips
½	cup firmly packed dark brown sugar
½	cup granulated sugar
½	cup canola oil
2	teaspoons pure vanilla extract
½	cup water

1. Line 2 baking sheets with parchment paper. In a large bowl, whisk together flour, cinnamon, baking soda, salt and nutmeg. Toss with oats and chocolate chips; set aside.

2. In a second bowl, break up brown sugar, making sure there are no lumps. Add granulated sugar, oil, vanilla and water, and whisk to combine. Add flour mixture and mix until just combined (there should be no streaks of flour). Scoop 2-inch mounds onto the prepared sheets, spacing them 2 inches apart. Freeze for 30 minutes.

3. Heat oven to 375°F. Bake, rotating the positions of the baking sheets after 6 minutes, until edges are golden brown, 9 to 12 minutes total. Let cool.

PER SERVING
About 285 calories, 16 g fat (6 g saturated fat), 4 g protein, 115 mg sodium, 34 g carbohydrates, 4 g fiber

≡ INGREDIENT ≡
SPOTLIGHT

Plant-Based Chocolate

Not all chocolate is vegan. Many bars and most semisweet chips include milk solids, so look for ones labeled "vegan" if you want to keep this recipe 100 percent plant-based.

GIFT IT!
Buy a cookie jar to fill with homemade
treats (two gifts in one!).

Mash-Up Cookies

Chocolate lovers, rejoice! These two-in-one cookies feature chocolate chips, white chocolate chips *and* cocoa powder. To turn them into a fun lunchbox treat, pipe "glasses" onto cookies using Decorator's Icing (page 25).

Active Time 25 minutes | **Total Time** 45 minutes, plus chilling | **Makes** 20

For the Chocolate Chip Cookie Dough

2 ¼	cups all-purpose flour
1	teaspoon baking soda
1	teaspoon kosher salt
1	cup (2 sticks) unsalted butter, at room temperature
½	cup packed light brown sugar
⅓	cup granulated sugar
2	large egg yolks
1	teaspoon pure vanilla extract
2	cups chocolate chips

For the Double Chocolate Cookie Dough

2	cups all-purpose flour
¾	cup unsweetened cocoa powder
1	teaspoon baking soda
1	teaspoon kosher salt
1	cup (2 sticks) unsalted butter, at room temperature
½	cup granulated sugar
⅓	cup packed light brown sugar
2	large egg yolks
1	teaspoon pure vanilla extract
2	cups white chocolate chips

1. Prepare both cookie doughs, making the chocolate chip first. (This way you won't have to clean the bowl between doughs.) In a large bowl, whisk together flour, cocoa powder (for the Double Chocolate Cookie Dough), baking soda and salt; set aside.

2. Using an electric mixer, beat together butter and sugars in another large bowl on medium speed until combined, 3 minutes. Add egg yolks and vanilla, and beat until just combined.

3. Reduce speed to low and add flour mixture until just combined. Fold in chocolate chips.

4. Heat oven to 350°F. Line 2 baking sheets with parchment paper.

5. Working one at a time, take 2 tablespoons each Chocolate Chip Cookie Dough and Double Chocolate Cookie Dough and press together to stick, then transfer to the prepared sheets, spacing them 2 inches apart. Freeze for 30 minutes.

6. Bake, rotating the positions of the baking sheets halfway through, until golden brown around edges, 15 to 20 minutes. Let cool on baking sheets for 5 minutes, then slide parchment (and cookies) onto cooling racks and cool for 5 minutes more before serving.

PER SERVING

About 525 calories, 30 g fat (19 g saturated fat), 6 g protein, 335 mg sodium, 62 g carbohydrates, 3 g fiber

Strawberry-Oatmeal Cookies

Fold in freeze-dried strawberries instead of classic raisins for a fun pink hue and some all-natural fruity sweetness.

Active Time 30 minutes | **Total Time** 45 minutes | **Makes** 24

1 ½   cups old-fashioned rolled oats

1 ¼   cups all-purpose flour

½   teaspoon baking soda

¼   teaspoon baking powder

½   teaspoon kosher salt

4   tablespoons (½ stick) unsalted butter, at room temperature

¾   cup packed light brown sugar

¼   cup granulated sugar

1   large egg, at room temperature

½   cup unsweetened applesauce, at room temperature

1   tablespoon pure vanilla extract

2   cups (2 ounces) freeze-dried strawberries, finely chopped

1. Heat oven to 350°F. Line 2 baking sheets with parchment paper. In a small bowl, whisk together oats, flour, baking soda, baking powder and salt; set aside.

2. Using an electric mixer, beat butter and sugars in a large bowl on high speed until light and fluffy, about 3 minutes.

3. Reduce speed to low and beat in egg until fully incorporated, then add applesauce and vanilla.

4. Gradually add flour mixture, mixing until just combined. Fold in strawberries.

5. Scoop balls of dough, about 2 tablespoons each, onto the prepared sheets, spacing them 2 inches apart. Bake until golden brown around edges but still soft in the middle, 12 to 16 minutes. Let cool on baking sheets for 4 minutes before serving or transferring to a cooling rack to cool.

PER SERVING

About 110 calories, 2.5 g fat (1.5 g saturated fat), 2 g protein, 75 mg sodium, 20 g carbohydrates, 1 g fiber

TEST
KITCHEN
TIP

Swap in freeze-dried raspberries, blueberries or mango pieces for different flavors.

Zucchini Bread Cookies

Scour the pantry for that half-eaten bag of pretzels, peanuts or any other munchies you have on hand and transform them into a delicious sweet 'n' salty snack.

Active Time 15 minutes | **Total Time** 40 minutes | **Makes** 24

3 1/3   cups all-purpose flour

1/3   cup cornstarch

1 1/2   teaspoons baking powder

1 1/4   teaspoons baking soda

1 1/2   teaspoons kosher salt

1 1/4   cups (2 1/2 sticks) unsalted butter, at room temperature

1 1/2   cups packed brown sugar

3/4   cup granulated sugar

2   large eggs

1   tablespoon pure vanilla extract

1   cup grated zucchini

3/4   cup chopped peanuts

3/4   cup broken pretzels

1. Heat oven to 350°F. Line 2 large baking sheets with parchment paper. In a medium bowl, whisk flour, cornstarch, baking powder, baking soda and salt; set aside.

2. Using an electric mixer, beat butter and sugars in a large bowl on medium speed until creamy, 3 minutes. Beat in eggs, one at a time until combined, then vanilla. Add flour mixture, stirring to combine. Fold in zucchini, peanuts and broken pretzels.

3. Drop scant 1/3 cupfuls of dough onto the prepared sheets, spacing them 1 inch apart. Bake until bottoms are golden brown, 20 to 25 minutes. Let cool on baking sheets on a cooling rack.

PER SERVING
About 275 calories, 13 g fat (7 g saturated fat), 4 g protein, 265 mg sodium, 38 g carbohydrates, 1 g fiber

---

Switch It Up!

Walnut Java Chip Cookies

Swap in **3/4 cup carrot peels** and **1/4 cup coffee grinds** for the zucchini and **3/4 cup chocolate chips** and **3/4 cup chopped walnuts** for the pretzels and peanuts.

Red Velvet Cookies

Studded with rich chocolate chips and colored a vibrant red, these cookies are inspired by the classic red velvet cake. This version skips the cream cheese frosting, but check out the bonus recipe below, just in case that's a deal breaker.

Active Time 20 minutes | **Total Time** 45 minutes | **Makes** 30

2	cups all-purpose flour
1/2	cup Dutch process cocoa powder
1	teaspoon baking soda
1	teaspoon kosher salt
1	cup (2 sticks) unsalted butter, at room temperature
3/4	cup packed brown sugar
1/2	cup granulated sugar
1	large egg
1	teaspoon red gel food coloring
2	teaspoons pure vanilla extract
2	cups semisweet chocolate chips

1. Heat oven to 350°F. Line 2 baking sheets with parchment paper. In a large bowl, whisk together flour, cocoa, baking soda and salt; set aside.

2. Using an electric mixer, beat together butter and sugars in a large bowl on medium speed until combined, about 3 minutes. Add egg, food coloring and vanilla, and mix until just combined.

3. Reduce speed to low and add flour mixture until just combined. Fold in chocolate chips.

4. Scoop heaping spoonfuls of dough onto the prepared sheets, spacing them 1 1/2 inches apart.

5. Bake, rotating the positions of the baking sheets halfway through, until darker around edges, 9 to 12 minutes total.

6. Let cool on baking sheets for 5 minutes, then slide parchment (and cookies) onto cooling racks and cool for at least 5 minutes more before serving.

PER SERVING

About 180 calories, 10 g fat (6 g saturated fat),
2 g protein, 115 mg sodium, 23 g carbohydrates, 2 g fiber

Bonus Recipe!

Cream Cheese Frosting

Using an electric mixer, beat together **8 ounces cream cheese, 1/2 cup unsalted butter** and **2 teaspoons pure vanilla extract** in a large bowl on medium-high speed until light and fluffy, 2 minutes. Reduce speed to low and beat in **16 ounces confectioners' sugar** until blended. Increase speed to medium-high and beat until light and creamy, 2 more minutes.

Dark Chocolate Candy Cookies

Sub in your favorite candy bar for plain chocolate to add personalized flavor to whatever you're baking — we used Matcha Kit Kats. (P.S. These cookies are a great way to work your way through your Halloween candy stash!)

Active Time 15 minutes | **Total Time** 1 hour | **Makes** 60

1 ¼	cups all-purpose flour
²∕₃	cup Dutch process cocoa powder
1	teaspoon baking powder
¼	teaspoon kosher salt
½	cup (1 stick) unsalted butter, at room temperature
¾	cup packed light brown sugar
¼	cup granulated sugar
1	large egg, at room temperature
1	teaspoon pure vanilla extract
2	ounces bittersweet chocolate, roughly chopped
12	mini Matcha Kit Kats, chopped

1. Heat oven to 350°F. Line 2 baking sheets with parchment paper. In a medium bowl, whisk together flour, cocoa, baking powder and salt; set aside.

2. Using an electric mixer, beat butter and sugars in a large bowl on medium speed until light and fluffy, about 3 minutes. Reduce speed to low and add egg and vanilla, then flour mixture, mixing until just incorporated. Fold in chopped chocolate and Kit Kats.

3. Drop 2 heaping tablespoonfuls of dough onto the prepared sheets, spacing them 2 inches apart, and refrigerate until chilled, at least 20 minutes.

4. Bake, rotating the positions of the baking sheets halfway through, until cookies are puffed and just set, 8 to 10 minutes. Let cool on baking sheets for 2 minutes before transferring to a cooling rack to cool completely.

PER SERVING
About 60 calories, 3 g fat (1 g saturated fat), 1 g protein, 20 mg sodium, 8 g carbohydrates, 1 g fiber

Cookie Cheat!

Here's an even easier way to transform that candy stockpile into one tasty treat: Spread **melted chocolate** onto a parchment-lined baking sheet and sprinkle with **chopped candy pieces**. Refrigerate until set. Break into pieces to enjoy. Done!

Peanut Butter & Candy Bar Thumbprints

Consider this an excuse to pick up an extra bag of mini candy bars whenever they're on sale.

Active Time 45 minutes | **Total Time** 1 hour 30 minutes, including cooling | **Makes** 36

1½   cups all-purpose flour

¾   teaspoon baking soda

½   teaspoon baking powder

½   teaspoon kosher salt

½   cup (1 stick) unsalted butter, at room temperature

¾   cup creamy peanut butter

⅓   cup granulated sugar

⅓   cup packed light brown sugar

1   large egg

1   teaspoon pure vanilla extract

½   cup sanding sugar

36   miniature chocolate candy bars, unwrapped

1. Heat oven to 375°F. Line 2 baking sheets with parchment paper. In a medium bowl, whisk together flour, baking soda, baking powder and salt; set aside.

2. Using an electric mixer, beat butter, peanut butter, granulated sugar and brown sugar in a large bowl on medium speed until light and creamy, 1 to 2 minutes. Beat in egg and then vanilla. Reduce speed to low and gradually add flour mixture, mixing until just combined.

3. Place sanding sugar in a small bowl. Scoop rounded tablespoonfuls of dough and drop them into sanding sugar, rolling to coat completely; transfer to the prepared sheets, spacing them 2 inches apart. Press thumb gently into center of each cookie to indent.

4. Bake, in batches, until bottoms are lightly browned, 8 to 10 minutes. Immediately press a candy bar into center of each cookie. Let cool on baking sheets on cooling racks for 10 minutes. Transfer cookies to cooling racks to cool completely.

PER SERVING
About 140 calories, 7 g fat (3 g saturated fat), 2 g protein, 100 mg sodium, 18 g carbohydrates, 1 g fiber

Classic Peanut Butter Cookies

Not too soft, not too sweet, these peanut butter buttons may be the simplest cookies you've ever made.

Active Time 25 minutes | **Total Time** 35 minutes
Makes 60

1 cup chunky or creamy peanut butter

¾ cup packed light brown sugar

1 large egg

¾ teaspoon baking soda

1. Heat oven to 350°F. Line 2 baking sheets with parchment paper.

2. Using an electric mixer, beat all ingredients in a large bowl on medium speed until fully incorporated, about 3 to 5 minutes.

3. Drop level teaspoonfuls of dough onto the prepared sheets, spacing them 1½ inches apart. Bake until the cookies are puffed and starting to lightly brown around edges, 8 to 10 minutes. Let cool on baking sheets for 5 minutes before transferring to a cooling rack to cool completely.

PER SERVING
About 35 calories, 2 g fat (0 g saturated fat), 1 g protein, 35 mg sodium, 3 g carbohydrates, 0 g fiber

Chunky Nut Butter Cookies

Swapping almond or cashew butter into the four-ingredient peanut butter cookies at left does not yield the same results. Enter this recipe. (See photo, at right.)

Active Time 15 minutes | **Total Time** 25 minutes
Makes 12

1 cup all-purpose flour

¼ teaspoon kosher salt

¼ teaspoon baking soda

⅓ cup plus 1 tablespoon nut butter (peanut, almond or cashew)

½ cup granulated sugar

⅓ cup packed light brown sugar

1 large egg

2 tablespoons cold water, plus more if necessary

1 teaspoon pure vanilla extract

¼ cup chopped nuts

1. Heat oven to 375°F. Line 2 baking sheets with parchment paper. In a medium bowl, whisk together flour, salt and baking soda; set aside.

2. Using an electric mixer, beat nut butter in a large bowl until smooth, about 1 minute. Mix in sugars, then add egg, 2 tablespoons water and vanilla, and beat until thick and glossy, 2 to 3 minutes.

3. Reduce speed to low, add flour mixture and mix until combined (if dough is crumbly, add 1 to 2 teaspoons water). Fold in nuts.

4. Drop 2 tablespoonfuls of dough onto the prepared sheets, spacing them 2 inches apart. Bake until puffed and turning golden brown around edges, 10 to 11 minutes. Transfer to a cooling rack to cool completely.

PER SERVING
About 170 calories, 6.5 g fat (1.5 g saturated fat), 4 g protein, 120 mg sodium, 25 g carbohydrates, 1 g fiber

Pistachio & Cherry Polvorones

These cookies, similar to Mexican wedding cookies, are coated in powdered sugar. They have chopped pistachios and cherries, but you can switch it up and use different nuts and dried fruit.

Active Time 1 hour 5 minutes | **Total Time** 1 hour 5 minutes, plus cooling | **Makes** 80

2	cups (4 sticks) unsalted butter, at room temperature
1	cup confectioners' sugar plus 1 ¼ cups for coating
2	tablespoons pure vanilla extract
1	teaspoon kosher salt
1	cup shelled unsalted pistachios (about 4 ounces), chopped
1	cup dried tart cherries or dried cranberries
3 ⅓	cups cake flour, sifted
1 ⅔	cups all-purpose flour, sifted

1. Heat oven to 350°F. Line 3 baking sheets with parchment paper. Using an electric mixer, beat butter and 1 cup sugar in a large bowl on medium speed until light and fluffy, 3 minutes. Mix in vanilla and salt, then pistachios and cherries. Stir in flours (do not overmix).

2. Working with one baking sheet at a time, shape dough into tablespoon-size balls and place onto the prepared sheet, spacing them 1 inch apart. Bake until bottoms just begin to turn golden brown, 15 to 16 minutes. Let cool on baking sheet for 10 minutes. Repeat with remaining dough.

3. Meanwhile, place remaining 1¼ cups sugar in a medium bowl. Working with 5 or 6 warm cookies at a time, gently coat in sugar. Transfer cookies to a piece of parchment paper to cool completely. Repeat with remaining cookies.

PER SERVING
About 100 calories, 5.5 g fat (3 g saturated fat), 1 g protein, 25 mg sodium, 12 g carbohydrates, 0 g fiber

Florentines

Lacy, crisp and chock-full of fruit and nuts, these delicate, chocolate-drizzled delights make cookie platters shine.

Active Time 40 minutes | **Total Time** 1 hour | **Makes** 66

1	cup raw pecans
5	tablespoons unsalted butter
¼	cup packed dark brown sugar
¼	cup honey
⅓	cup all-purpose flour
¼	teaspoon kosher salt
¼	cup dried cranberries, finely chopped
¼	cup candied ginger, finely chopped
1	teaspoon finely grated orange zest
1	cup bittersweet chocolate chips

1. Heat oven to 375°F. Line 2 baking sheets with parchment paper. Using a food processor, pulse pecans until finely chopped but not powdery, with some small chunks remaining.

2. In a medium saucepan, combine butter, brown sugar and honey, and cook on medium, stirring occasionally, until butter has melted, sugar has dissolved and mixture is smooth, 8 minutes. Remove from heat and stir in flour and salt, then chopped pecans. Fold in cranberries, ginger and zest.

3. Drop leveled teaspoonfuls of batter onto the prepared sheets, spacing them 3 inches apart. Bake until golden brown, about 5 to 7 minutes. Let cool on baking sheets until set, about 8 minutes, before transferring to cooling racks to cool completely. Repeat with remaining dough.

4. In a small bowl, microwave chocolate at 50 percent power in 30-second intervals, stirring in between, until melted and smooth.

5. Place cooled cookies on a piece of parchment paper and drizzle with melted chocolate. Let sit until chocolate is set.

PER SERVING

About 125 calories, 8 g fat (3 g saturated fat), 1 g protein, 20 mg sodium, 12 g carbohydrates, 0.5 g fiber

Pimiento Cheese Thumbprints

These cheesy thumbprint biscuits, filled with a red currant jelly, are proof that savory cookies can be crowd-pleasers too.

Active Time 30 minutes | **Total Time** 50 minutes | **Makes** 40

8 ounces sharp orange Cheddar, coarsely grated

1½ cups all-purpose flour

½ teaspoon mustard powder

½ teaspoon kosher salt

2 tablespoons chopped pimientos or roasted red peppers

½ teaspoon Tabasco

½ cup (1 stick) unsalted butter, cold and cut into cubes

¼ cup red currant jelly

TEST KITCHEN TIP

Not planning to eat these right away? Simply store the cookies and jam separately, then fill the cookies with jam right before serving.

1. Line 2 baking sheets with parchment paper.

2. In a food processor, pulse together Cheddar, flour, mustard powder and salt until combined. Pulse in pimientos and Tabasco. Add butter and pulse until coarse crumbs form.

3. Transfer dough to a bowl. If dough is dry, add water, 1 teaspoon at a time, until dough holds together when squeezed. Using your hands, roll dough into 1-inch balls, press thumb into centers to leave deep indents, and place onto the prepared sheets. Refrigerate until very firm, at least 30 minutes or up to 3 days.

4. Heat oven to 375°F. Bake, rotating the positions of the baking sheets halfway through, until light golden brown around edges, 18 to 22 minutes.

5. Transfer to cooling racks to cool completely. Once cool and when ready to serve, spoon jam into center of each cookie.

PER SERVING

About 65 calories, 4 g fat (2.5 g saturated fat), 2 g protein, 60 mg sodium, 5 g carbohydrates, 0 g fiber

Glazed Sourdough Snickerdoodles

You don't need a sourdough starter to make these cookies. Buttermilk, cream of tartar and apple cider vinegar add enough tang to balance out the sweetness of the cinnamon-sugar dough.

Active Time 30 minutes | **Total Time** 1 hour 15 minutes | **Makes** 18

For the Cookies

1	cup all-purpose flour
¼	cup whole-wheat flour
1	teaspoon cream of tartar
⅛	teaspoon kosher salt
½	cup (1 stick) unsalted butter, at room temperature
½	cup granulated sugar
¼	cup packed brown sugar
1	large egg
1	tablespoon buttermilk
½	teaspoon apple cider vinegar

For the Spiced Sugar

⅓	cup granulated sugar
1½	teaspoons ground cinnamon
1½	teaspoons ground ginger
¼	teaspoon freshly grated nutmeg

For the Sour Cream Glaze

1¼	cups confectioners' sugar
3	tablespoons sour cream

1. Line 2 baking sheets with parchment paper.

2. Make the cookies: In a medium bowl, whisk together flours, cream of tartar and salt; set aside. Using an electric mixer, beat butter and sugars in a large bowl on medium speed until light and fluffy, 3 minutes. Reduce speed to low and beat in egg, followed by buttermilk and vinegar. Mix in flour mixture until just incorporated.

3. Make the spiced sugar: In a small bowl, whisk together sugar, cinnamon, ginger and nutmeg.

4. Scoop rounded tablespoonfuls of dough, dropping dough into spiced sugar to coat completely before transferring to the prepared sheets. Freeze until firm, about 30 minutes.

5. Heat oven to 350°F. Bake, rotating the positions of the baking sheets after 9 minutes, until cookies are puffed and edges are light golden brown, 12 to 14 minutes total. Transfer to cooling racks.

6. Prepare the glaze: In a small bowl, whisk together confectioners' sugar and sour cream. (At first it may not seem like there is enough liquid, but it will eventually come together.) Using the tip of a knife or a small piping bag, glaze cookies by drawing lines back and forth on a diagonal across the surface. Let glaze set.

PER SERVING
About 165 calories, 6 g fat (3.5 g saturated fat), 1 g protein, 25 mg sodium, 28 g carbohydrates, 1 g fiber

Pecan Shortbread Cookies

Roasted pecans and turbinado sugar make these shortbread cookies a sweet and nutty treat.

Active Time 40 minutes | **Total Time** 1 hour 20 minutes, plus chilling | **Makes** 36

2 cups plus 1 cup pecan halves

1 cup (2 sticks) unsalted butter, at room temperature

½ cup granulated sugar

1 teaspoon pure vanilla extract

½ teaspoon kosher salt

2 ¼ cups all-purpose flour

½ cup turbinado sugar

1. Heat oven to 350°F. Line 2 baking sheets with parchment paper. Spread 2 cups pecans onto a baking sheet and toast until just fragrant, 7 to 8 minutes. Let cool, then chop.

2. Using an electric mixer, beat butter, granulated sugar, vanilla and salt in a large bowl on medium speed until light and fluffy, 3 minutes. Reduce speed to low and mix in flour, one large spoonful at a time, until just combined. Add chopped pecans and mix until incorporated. Cover and refrigerate for at least 1 hour or up to 24 hours.

3. Place turbinado sugar in a small bowl. Divide dough into 36 balls, each 1¼ inches. Roll balls in turbinado sugar and then place onto the prepared sheets, spacing them 2 inches apart. Gently press remaining pecans into the top of each cookie. Bake, rotating the positions of the baking sheets once, until edges are golden brown, 15 to 17 minutes. Let cool on baking sheets on cooling racks for 5 minutes before transferring to racks to cool completely.

PER SERVING

About 155 calories, 11 g fat (4 g saturated fat), 2 g protein, 30 mg sodium, 13 g carbohydrates, 1 g fiber

Razzy Jammy Thumbprints

Taking a cue from the Swedish pastry Hallongrotta (a.k.a. "raspberry cave"), this jammy cookie recipe adds a touch of honey to the dough.

Active Time 25 minutes | **Total Time** 40 minutes, plus cooling | **Makes** 36

2 ¼	cups all-purpose flour
1	teaspoon baking powder
½	teaspoon baking soda
¾	cup (1½ sticks) unsalted butter, at room temperature
¾	cups granulated sugar
½	teaspoon kosher salt
1	large egg yolk
2	tablespoons honey
1	teaspoon pure almond extract
½	teaspoon pure vanilla extract
½	cup seedless raspberry jam
¼	cup confectioners' sugar, optional

Switch It Up!

Salted Caramel Thumbprints

Bake cookies unfilled. Once cooled, fill with **dulce de leche** and top with **flaky sea salt**.

1. Heat oven to 375°F. Line 2 baking sheets with parchment paper. In a medium bowl, whisk flour, baking powder and baking soda; set aside.

2. Using an electric mixer, beat butter, granulated sugar and salt in a large bowl on medium-high speed until creamy, 3 minutes. Beat in egg yolk, then honey and extracts until smooth, stopping and scraping down the side of the bowl occasionally. Reduce speed to low, then mix in flour mixture until smooth.

3. Roll tablespoonfuls of dough into balls and place onto the prepared sheets, spacing them 2 inches apart. With a floured finger or the rounded end of a small spoon, make an indentation in the center of each ball. Fill each indentation with ½ teaspoon jam. Bake until golden brown around edges, 12 minutes.

4. Let cool on baking sheets for 5 minutes before transferring to a cooling rack to cool completely. Sift confectioners' sugar over cooled cookies if desired. Cookies can be stored in airtight containers in the freezer for up to a month.

PER SERVING

About 95 calories, 4 g fat (3 g saturated fat), 1 g protein, 95 mg sodium, 14 g carbohydrates, 0 g fiber

Caramel, Chocolate & Walnut Thumbprints

Featuring bourbon, homemade caramel, melted chocolate and toasted walnuts, these butter cookies take inspiration from Kentucky's famous Derby Pie but are delicious any time of year.

Active Time 25 minutes | **Total Time** 50 minutes | **Makes** 28

2 1/2 cups all-purpose flour, plus more for shaping

1/2 teaspoon baking powder

1 1/2 teaspoons kosher salt

1 cup (2 sticks) plus 1 tablespoon unsalted butter, at room temperature

1 3/4 cups sugar

1 large egg yolk

1 teaspoon pure vanilla extract

1/4 cup water

1/3 cup heavy cream

2 tablespoons bourbon

1/2 cup chopped toasted walnuts

1/2 cup semisweet chocolate chips

Switch It Up!

Check out the brownie version of Derby Pie (page 207).

1. Heat oven to 350°F. Line 2 baking sheets with parchment paper. In a large bowl, whisk together flour, baking powder and 1/2 teaspoon salt; set aside.

2. Using an electric mixer, beat 1 cup butter and 3/4 cup sugar in a separate large bowl on medium speed until light and fluffy, 1 to 2 minutes. Add egg and vanilla, and beat until combined, 1 minute. Reduce speed to low and gradually add flour mixture, mixing until just combined.

3. Roll heaping tablespoonfuls of dough into balls and place onto the prepared sheets, spacing them 2 inches apart. Dip the bottom of a 1/2 teaspoon measuring spoon in flour and press into each cookie to make a thumbprint. Refrigerate for 30 minutes.

4. Bake until golden brown, 16 to 19 minutes. Use 1/2 teaspoon measuring spoon to reshape thumbprints. Transfer to a cooling rack to let cool.

5. In a medium saucepan, combine water and remaining 1 cup sugar and cook on medium-low, stirring, until sugar has dissolved, 3 to 4 minutes. Once dissolved, stop stirring and cook until deep golden brown, 10 to 12 minutes. Remove from heat and carefully stir in cream and bourbon. Add remaining 1 teaspoon salt and 1 tablespoon butter; swirl until dissolved. Transfer to a bowl and let cool for 5 minutes. Stir in walnuts and chocolate chips until chips are melted. Let sit for 10 minutes.

6. Fill thumbprints with caramel mixture, dividing evenly.

PER SERVING
About 195 calories, 11 g fat (6 g saturated fat), 2 g protein, 115 mg sodium, 24 g carbohydrates, 1 g fiber

Candied Ginger & Citrus Kitchen Sink Cookies

Many kitchen sink cookies feature crushed potato chips or pretzels, toffee bits and chocolate chips. This version is packed with chewy candied ginger, orange peel and pistachios — a flavor profile that is unexpected yet divine.

Active Time 35 minutes | **Total Time** 1 hour | **Makes** 60

1	cup plus 2 tablespoons all-purpose flour
½	teaspoon baking soda
¼	teaspoon kosher salt
	Pinch ground ginger
	Pinch ground cloves
½	cup (1 stick) unsalted butter, at room temperature
⅔	cup packed brown sugar
¼	cup granulated sugar
1	large egg
1	teaspoon dark rum or pure vanilla extract
¾	cup chopped pecans
2	tablespoons chopped candied ginger
6	tablespoons chopped candied orange peel
6	tablespoons chopped pistachios

1. Line 3 baking sheets with parchment paper. In a medium bowl, whisk together flour, baking soda, salt and ground ginger and cloves; set aside.

2. Using an electric mixer, beat butter and sugars in a large bowl on medium speed until light and fluffy, about 3 minutes. Beat in egg, then rum (or vanilla), and mix for 2 minutes. Reduce speed to low and gradually add flour mixture until nearly combined. Add pecans, candied ginger and 4 tablespoons each orange peel and pistachios.

3. Scoop rounded teaspoonfuls of dough onto the prepared sheets, spacing them 1½ inches apart. Press remaining candied orange peel and pistachios into top of each cookie. Freeze until firm, about 15 minutes.

4. Heat oven to 375°F. Bake, rotating the positions of the baking sheets after 8 minutes, until edges begin to turn golden brown, 11 to 12 minutes total. Let cool.

PER SERVING
About 55 calories, 3 g fat (1 g saturated fat), 1 g protein, 20 mg sodium, 7 g carbohydrates, 0 g fiber

GIFT IT!
Dress up plain tins with colorful
issue paper and festive ribbon.

Chewy Chocolate-Walnut Cookies

Crunchy on the outside and chewy on the inside, these simple cookies are easily customized with your choice of chips — peanut butter, milk, dark or white chocolate. (See photo, page 32.)

Active Time 10 minutes | **Total Time** 30 minutes | **Makes** 15

Nonstick cooking spray, for the pan

3 cups confectioners' sugar

¾ cup Dutch process cocoa powder

½ teaspoon kosher salt

2 large eggs, at room temperature

1 teaspoon pure vanilla extract

1 cup toasted walnuts, chopped

½ cup bittersweet or dark chocolate chips

Flaky sea salt

1. Heat oven to 350°F. Line 2 baking sheets with parchment paper and lightly coat with cooking spray.

2. In a medium bowl, whisk together sugar, cocoa powder and salt; set aside.

3. Using an electric mixer, mix together eggs and vanilla in a large bowl. Add sugar mixture and mix to combine; fold in walnuts and chocolate chips.

4. Spoon mounds of dough (about 1½ tablespoons per cookie) onto the prepared sheets, spacing them 2 inches apart, and sprinkle with flaky sea salt.

5. Bake, rotating the positions of the baking sheets once, until cookies are puffed and tops begin to crack, 12 to 14 minutes. Let cool on baking sheets for 5 minutes, then slide parchment (and cookies) onto a cooling rack to cool completely.

PER SERVING

About 210 calories, 8.5 g fat (2.5 g saturated fat), 3 g protein, 270 mg sodium, 31 g carbohydrates, 2 g fiber

Pumpkin-Cherry Cookies

Yes, you *can* have cookies for breakfast! These delicious on-the-go treats, at left, are packed with protein (and fiber!) to keep you energized till noon.

Active Time 15 minutes | **Total Time** 45 minutes | **Makes** 16

2	cups whole-wheat flour
1	cup old-fashioned oats
1	teaspoon baking soda
1	teaspoon pumpkin pie spice
½	teaspoon kosher salt
1	15-ounce can pure pumpkin
1	cup olive oil
1	cup packed brown sugar
1	large egg
½	cup roasted salted pepitas
½	cup dried cherries

1. Heat oven to 350°F. Line 2 baking sheets with parchment paper. In a medium bowl, whisk together flour, oats, baking soda, pumpkin pie spice and salt; set aside.

2. Using an electric mixer, mix pumpkin, oil, sugar and egg in a large bowl on medium speed to combine, 1 to 2 minutes. Reduce speed to low; gradually incorporate flour mixture, then pepitas and cherries.

3. Scoop 16 mounds (about ⅓ cup each) onto the prepared sheets, spacing them 2 inches apart; flatten into disks. Bake until dark golden brown on bottom, 20 to 25 minutes. Transfer to a cooling rack to cool completely.

PER SERVING
About 290 calories, 16.5 g fat (2.5 g saturated fat), 4 g protein, 160 mg sodium, 33 g carbohydrates, 3 g fiber

TEST KITCHEN TIP

Store cookies in an airtight container for up to 2 days or freeze for up to 2 weeks. Reheat in the toaster until crisp.

Triple-Chocolate Hazelnut Cookies

Bake up a batch (or three!) of these cookies for all the Nutella lovers in your life. They are packed with rich chocolatey flavor and studded with toasted hazelnuts.

Active Time 20 minutes | **Total Time** 1 hour 45 minutes | **Makes** 48

3 1/2	cups all-purpose flour
1	cup granulated sugar
1	cup packed light brown sugar
2	teaspoons baking powder
1	teaspoon kosher salt
1/2	teaspoon baking soda
1/2	teaspoon instant coffee powder
1	cup cocoa powder
3/4	cup canola oil
3/4	cup chocolate-hazelnut spread
3/4	cup warm water
2	large eggs, at room temperature
1	teaspoon pure vanilla extract
1 1/2	cups coarsely chopped bittersweet chocolate
1	cup coarsely chopped toasted hazelnuts
2	teaspoons flaky sea salt

1. Heat oven to 350°F with the racks in the upper and lower thirds. Line 2 baking sheets with parchment paper. In a large bowl, whisk together flour, sugars, baking powder, salt, baking soda and coffee; set aside.

2. Using an electric mixer, mix cocoa, oil, chocolate-hazelnut spread and water in another large bowl on low speed until combined, about 30 seconds. Add eggs, one at a time, beating until incorporated after each addition. Mix in vanilla. Stir flour mixture into cocoa mixture until just incorporated. Stir in chocolate and hazelnuts.

3. Scoop mounds of dough (about 2 tablespoons per cookie) onto the prepared sheets, spacing them 3 inches apart. Sprinkle cookies with sea salt. Bake, rotating the positions of the baking sheets halfway through, until dry around edges, 12 to 14 minutes. Let cool on baking sheets on cooling racks for 10 minutes before transferring cookies to the racks to cool completely. Repeat with remaining dough.

PER SERVING

About 180 calories, 10 g fat (4 g saturated fat), 3 g protein, 180 mg sodium, 24 g carbohydrates, 2 g fiber

---

Bonus Recipe!

Chocolate-Hazelnut Spread

Roast **1 cup hazelnuts** on a rimmed baking sheet in a 375°F oven for 10 minutes, shaking once or twice. Wrap hot hazelnuts in a towel and roll vigorously to remove peel; cool completely. In a food processor, process peeled hazelnuts and **1/2 teaspoon kosher salt** until mostly smooth and runny, about 8 minutes. In a medium bowl, melt **3 1/2 ounces dark chocolate, chopped**, in the microwave in 20-second intervals; stir in **1 cup sweetened condensed milk** and **2 tablespoons light corn syrup**. Add chocolate mixture to pureed hazelnuts; pulse until just combined. Makes about 2 cups.

GIFT IT!
Stack four cookies in a clear cellophane bag,
then tie decorative ribbon at each end of the bag to cinch.
Trim the ends and then add a metal-rim tag.

S'more Cookies

Bring the classic campfire treat indoors! Here, summer's favorite dessert ingredients are transformed into a delectably ooey-gooey cookie.

Active Time 30 minutes | **Total Time** 1 hour 10 minutes | **Makes** 18

2	cups all-purpose flour
10	graham crackers, crushed to fine crumbs
1	teaspoon baking soda
1	teaspoon kosher salt
1	cup (2 sticks) unsalted butter, at room temperature
½	cup granulated sugar
½	cup packed dark brown sugar
1	teaspoon pure vanilla extract
2	large eggs
1⅓	cups dark chocolate chips
2	cups marshmallow cream
2¼	teaspoons flaky sea salt

1. Heat oven to 350°F. Line 2 baking sheets with parchment paper.

2. In a large bowl, whisk together flour, graham cracker crumbs, baking soda and salt; set aside.

3. Using an electric mixer, beat butter and sugars in a large bowl on medium speed until light and fluffy, about 3 minutes. Add vanilla and eggs, one at a time, beating each until fully incorporated before adding the next. Add flour mixture and mix until just combined.

4. Drop mounds of dough (2 tablespoons per cookie) onto the prepared sheets, spacing them 2 inches apart. Lightly press down with the palm of your hand to flatten to ½ inch thick. Bake until golden brown around edges, 14 to 15 minutes. Let cool on baking sheets for 5 minutes before transferring cookies to a cooling rack to cool completely.

5. In a small heatproof bowl set over a small saucepan of simmering water, melt chocolate until smooth, stirring often. Let cool 2 to 4 minutes. Using a spoon or small spatula, spread each cookie with 1 heaping teaspoon marshmallow cream. Drizzle 1 teaspoon melted chocolate on top and swirl together. Sprinkle immediately with sea salt. Let set for 30 minutes.

PER SERVING
About 350 calories, 17 g fat (10 g saturated fat), 4 g protein, 525 mg sodium, 44 g carbohydrates, 2 g fiber

Frosted Lemon Ricotta Cookies

For anyone who is a fan of a cakier cookie, you can't do better than this light and fluffy number. Instead of rainbow nonpareils, they are finished off with an icy blue glaze and edible silver stars, making them a kid favorite.

Active Time 30 minutes | **Total Time** 1 hour, plus cooling | **Makes** 42

4	cups all-purpose flour
2	teaspoons baking powder
1	teaspoon kosher salt
1 3/4	cups granulated sugar
1	cup (2 sticks) unsalted butter, at room temperature
1	teaspoon lemon zest plus 3 tablespoons juice
1	15-ounce container ricotta cheese
2	large eggs
2	teaspoons pure vanilla extract
1 1/4	cups confectioners' sugar
1/2	teaspoon water
	Blue food coloring, for decorating
	Edible silver stars, for decorating

1. Heat oven to 350°F. In a large bowl, whisk flour, baking powder and salt; set aside.

2. Using an electric mixer, beat granulated sugar, butter and lemon zest in another large bowl on medium-high speed until creamy, 3 minutes. Add ricotta, eggs and vanilla, beating until combined, stopping and scraping down the side of the bowl occasionally. Mix in flour mixture until just smooth.

3. Line a large baking sheet with parchment paper. With a small cookie scoop (about 2 teaspoons), scoop dough into balls and place onto the prepared sheet, spacing them 1 1/2 inches apart. With your fingers, pat each down into a disk. Bake until bottoms are golden brown, 15 to 20 minutes. Let cool on baking sheet for 5 minutes before transferring to a cooling rack to cool completely.

4. Make the glaze: In a medium bowl, stir together confectioners' sugar, reserved lemon juice and water, until smooth. Tint with food coloring to desired shade. Place in a small resealable plastic bag with one corner snipped off and drizzle all over cookies. Decorate with edible stars if desired. Let sit until set, about 30 minutes. Cookies can be stored in airtight containers in the freezer for up to a month.

PER SERVING
About 150 calories, 6 g fat (4 g saturated fat), 3 g protein, 130 mg sodium, 22 g carbohydrates, 0 g fiber

---

Switch It Up!

Chocolate-Glazed Ricotta Cookies

Omit lemon in cookies. Instead of confectioners' sugar glaze, drizzle with **melted dark chocolate**.

Spiced Drops

Sometimes a little spice adds a whole lot of sophistication. In this twist on a snickerdoodle, you'll fold spices like ginger and cloves into the dough, adding an extra layer of flavor.

Active Time 35 minutes | **Total Time** 55 minutes, plus chilling and cooling | **Makes** 42

2 ¼	cups all-purpose flour
2 ½	teaspoons ground cinnamon
2	teaspoons ground ginger
¼	teaspoon ground cloves
1	teaspoon baking powder
½	teaspoon baking soda
¾	cups (1 ½ sticks) unsalted butter, at room temperature
¾	cups granulated sugar
½	teaspoon kosher salt
1	large egg yolk
2	tablespoons light corn syrup
1 ½	teaspoons pure vanilla extract
½	teaspoon pure almond extract
¼	cup coarse sugar

1. Heat oven to 375°F. Line a baking sheet with parchment paper. In a medium bowl, whisk flour, cinnamon, ginger, cloves, baking powder and baking soda; set aside.

2. Using an electric mixer, beat butter, sugar and salt in a large bowl on medium-high speed until light and fluffy, about 3 minutes. Beat in egg yolk, corn syrup and extracts. Reduce speed to medium-low and mix in flour mixture until just combined.

3. Place coarse sugar in a small bowl. Roll tablespoonfuls of dough into balls, then roll in sugar and place onto the prepared sheet, spacing them 2 inches apart.

4. Bake until edges are set, 15 minutes. Slide the parchment with cookies onto a cooling rack to cool completely.

PER SERVING
About 80 calories, 4 g fat (2 g saturated fat), 1 g protein, 55 mg sodium, 11 g carbohydrates, 0 g fiber

Pignoli Cookies

Also known as pine nut cookies, these meringue-like Italian confections are crisp on the outside and soft on the inside.

Active Time 30 minutes | **Total Time** 1 hour | **Makes** 24

1	7-ounce tube almond paste, coarsely crumbled
¾	cup confectioners' sugar
1	large egg white
1	tablespoon plus 1 teaspoon honey
⅓	cup pine nuts

1. Heat oven to 350°F. Line several baking sheets with parchment paper. In a food processor with a knife blade attached, blend crumbled almond paste and confectioners' sugar until mixture resembles fine crumbs.

2. Using an electric mixer, beat almond paste mixture, egg white and honey in a large bowl on medium speed until blended, 2 to 3 minutes. Increase speed to high; beat until very smooth, occasionally scraping the bowl with a rubber spatula, 5 minutes (mixture will be thick).

3. Spoon almond mixture into a large piping bag with a large round tip. Pipe 1¼-inch rounds onto the prepared sheets, spacing them 2 inches apart. With a moistened fingertip, gently smooth surface of cookies. Sprinkle with pine nuts; lightly press to cover tops of cookies.

4. Bake until nuts are golden brown and cookies are lightly golden brown around edges, 10 to 12 minutes. Let cool on baking sheets for 5 minutes before transferring to a cooling rack to cool completely. Repeat with remaining almond mixture. Store cookies in tightly covered containers for up to 2 weeks.

PER SERVING
About 70 calories, 3 g fat (0 g saturated fat), 2 g protein, 5 mg sodium, 9 g carbohydrates, 0 g fiber

Potato Chip & Pecan Sandies

Introducing the best way to use up all the crushed chips and crumbs left behind in the bottom of the bag.

Active Time 20 minutes | **Total Time** 45 minutes | **Makes** 30

¾	cup (1 ½ sticks) unsalted butter, at room temperature
1	teaspoon pure vanilla extract
¼	teaspoon kosher salt
¾	cup granulated sugar
1½	cups all-purpose flour
½	cup pecans, chopped
¾	cup crushed potato chips

1. Heat oven to 350°F. Line 2 baking sheets with parchment paper.

2. Using an electric mixer, beat butter, vanilla, salt and ½ cup sugar in a large bowl on medium speed until light and fluffy, about 3 minutes. Reduce speed to low and mix in flour, mixing until just incorporated. Stir in pecans and crushed potato chips.

3. In a small bowl, place remaining ¼ cup sugar. Roll level tablespoonfuls of dough into balls and then roll in sugar to coat. Place balls onto the prepared sheets, spacing them 2 inches apart. With a flat-bottomed measuring cup or glass, press each ball into a ¼-inch-thick disk. Bake until lightly golden brown, 16 to 18 minutes. Let cool on baking sheets for 5 minutes before transferring to a cooling rack to cool completely.

PER SERVING
About 115 calories, 7 g fat (3 g saturated fat), 1 g protein, 35 mg sodium, 12 g carbohydrates, 1 g fiber

Mini "Black & White" Cookies

An homage to the classic black-and-white cookies popular in New York City, these bites play up pretty pastels — but feel free to make them whatever colors you please!

Active Time 30 minutes | **Total Time** 1 hour, plus cooling | **Makes** 36

For the Cookies

2	cups all-purpose flour
1/2	teaspoon baking soda
1/4	teaspoon kosher salt
3/4	cups (1 1/2 sticks) unsalted butter, at room temperature
1	cup granulated sugar
2	large eggs
1/2	cup buttermilk

For the Icing

1	pound confectioners' sugar
2	tablespoons light corn syrup
2	tablespoons whole milk
1/8	teaspoon kosher salt
	Assorted food colorings

1. Heat oven to 350°F. Line 2 baking sheets with parchment paper.

2. Make the cookies: In a medium bowl, whisk together flour, baking soda and salt; set aside. Using an electric mixer, beat butter and granulated sugar in a large bowl on medium speed until fluffy, 3 minutes. Beat in eggs one at a time. Reduce speed to low, add flour mixture alternately with buttermilk, beginning and ending with flour mixture.

3. Drop rounded tablespoonfuls of dough onto the prepared sheets, spacing them 2 inches apart. Bake, rotating the positions of the baking sheets halfway through, until golden brown, 13 to 15 minutes; let cool.

4. Meanwhile, make the icing: Using an electric mixer, beat confectioners' sugar, corn syrup, milk and salt in a medium bowl on low speed until smooth. Divide icing evenly into 2 bowls and tint with food coloring as desired. Spread icing on flat side of each cookie; let set 30 minutes.

PER SERVING

About 140 calories, 4 g fat (3 g saturated fat), 1 g protein, 75 mg sodium, 25 g carbohydrates, 0 g fiber

Ginger Crinkles

Molasses makes these cookies extra soft and chewy, and pairs beautifully with fresh ginger.

Active Time 30 minutes | **Total Time** 1 hour 30 minutes | **Makes** 72

2 ¾ cups all-purpose flour

1 teaspoon baking powder

1 teaspoon baking soda

¼ teaspoon kosher salt

¾ cup (1 ½ sticks) unsalted butter, at room temperature

1 ½ cups granulated sugar

1 large egg

¼ cup molasses

1 tablespoon freshly grated ginger

TEST KITCHEN TIP

To easily peel ginger, use the edge of a spoon to scrape away the thin skin.

1. Heat oven to 350°F. Line 2 baking sheets with parchment paper. In a medium bowl, whisk together flour, baking powder, baking soda and salt; set aside.

2. Using an electric mixer, beat butter and 1 cup sugar in a large bowl on medium speed until light and fluffy, about 3 minutes. Beat in egg, molasses and ginger. Reduce speed to low and gradually add flour mixture, mixing until just incorporated (dough will be soft). Refrigerate until firm enough to handle, about 1 hour.

3. Place remaining ½ cup sugar in a small bowl. Roll half the dough into 1-inch balls (about 1 rounded teaspoon each) and then roll in sugar to coat. Place balls onto the prepared sheets, spacing them 2 inches apart.

4. Bake, rotating the positions of the baking sheets halfway through, until cookies are puffed, cracked and set, 8 to 10 minutes. Let cool on baking sheets for 2 minutes before transferring to a cooling rack to cool completely. Repeat with remaining dough.

PER SERVING

About 55 calories, 2 g fat (1 g saturated fat), 1 g protein, 30 mg sodium, 9 g carbohydrates, 0 g fiber

Red Velvet Snowballs

Inspired by the forever-favorite snowball cookie, these red velvet morsels are rolled in powdered sugar not once but twice.

Active Time 20 minutes | **Total Time** 1 hour 40 minutes | **Makes** 24

2 ½ cups all-purpose flour

¼ cup cocoa powder

2 teaspoons baking powder

¼ teaspoon kosher salt

¾ cup (1 ½ sticks) unsalted butter, at room temperature

3 cups confectioners' sugar

1 tablespoon red food coloring

1 teaspoon pure vanilla extract

1 teaspoon white vinegar

1. Heat oven to 350°F with racks in the upper and lower thirds. Line 2 baking sheets with parchment paper. In a large bowl, whisk together flour, cocoa, baking powder and salt; set aside.

2. Using an electric mixer, beat butter and 1½ cups confectioners' sugar in a large bowl on medium speed until smooth, 1 to 2 minutes. Reduce speed to low and gradually add flour mixture, mixing until just incorporated, 1 to 2 minutes. Add food coloring, vanilla and vinegar; increase speed to medium and mix just until dough forms large crumbs, 15 to 20 seconds.

3. Shape dough into balls (about 2 tablespoons each). Place balls onto the prepared sheets, spacing them 1 inch apart; freeze for 10 minutes. Bake, rotating the positions of the baking sheets halfway through, until cookies are dry around edges, 15 to 18 minutes. Let cool on baking sheets on a cooling rack for 5 minutes.

4. Place remaining 1½ cups confectioners' sugar in a bowl. Working one at a time, gently toss warm cookies in sugar to coat. Return cookies to baking sheets to cool completely; reserve remaining sugar. Once cool, toss again, in batches, in remaining sugar.

PER SERVING

About 160 calories, 6 g fat (4 g saturated fat), 2 g protein, 70 mg sodium, 26 g carbohydrates, 1 g fiber

GIFT IT!
Fill a six-egg carton with mini cupcake liners,
then add cookies. Tie it up with a pretty ribbon.

Black & Red Crinkle Cookies

The secret to this cookie's gorgeous-meets-mysterious appearance? Dark black cocoa powder, which adds color as well as a depth of rich chocolate flavor to red velvet dough.

Active Time 15 minutes | **Total Time** 1 hour | **Makes** 36

1½ cups all-purpose flour

2 tablespoons unsweetened cocoa powder, plus more for coating

1 teaspoon baking powder

½ teaspoon kosher salt

½ teaspoon cinnamon

1¼ cups granulated sugar

4 tablespoons (½ stick) unsalted butter, melted

½ teaspoon red gel food coloring

1 teaspoon pure vanilla extract

2 large eggs

1. In a medium bowl, sift together flour, cocoa powder, baking powder, salt and cinnamon; set aside.

2. In a large bowl, whisk together sugar, butter, food coloring, vanilla and eggs. Fold flour mixture into sugar mixture until smooth. Cover bowl with plastic wrap and refrigerate until chilled, about 30 minutes (it will still be soft).

3. Heat oven to 375°F. Line 2 baking sheets with parchment paper.

4. Place some cocoa powder in a shallow bowl. Roll tablespoonfuls of dough into balls, then completely coat in cocoa and transfer to the prepared sheets, spacing them 3 inches apart.

5. Bake until cookies are slightly firm to the touch, about 12 to 14 minutes. Let cool on baking sheets for 10 minutes. Repeat with remaining dough.

PER SERVING

About 65 calories, 2 g fat (1 g saturated fat), 1 g protein, 50 mg sodium, 12 g carbohydrates, 0 g fiber

Chocolate Crinkle Cookies

Here is your classic crinkle cookie recipe — complete with melt-in-your-mouth chocolatey goodness, hits of sugary sweetness and a chew you can appreciate with every single bite.

Active Time 25 minutes | **Total Time** 45 minutes, plus chilling | **Makes** 48

1½   cups all-purpose flour

½   cup unsweetened cocoa

1½   teaspoons baking powder

¼   teaspoon kosher salt

½   cup (1 stick) unsalted butter, at room temperature

1   cup firmly packed dark brown sugar

2   large eggs

1   teaspoon pure vanilla extract

4   ounces bittersweet chocolate, chopped, melted and cooled

½   cup confectioners' sugar

TEST KITCHEN TIP

Roll cookies, freeze for up to 3 months and then bake (from frozen) as directed.

1. Line 2 baking sheets with parchment paper. In a medium bowl, whisk together flour, cocoa, baking powder and salt; set aside.

2. Using an electric mixer, beat butter and brown sugar in a large bowl on medium speed until light and fluffy, about 3 minutes. Beat in eggs and vanilla, then cooled chocolate. Reduce speed to low and gradually add flour mixture, mixing until just incorporated.

3. Place confectioners' sugar in a small bowl. Drop a slightly heaping tablespoonful of dough into confectioners' sugar (the dough will be soft) and roll to coat and form into a ball; repeat with remaining dough. Place the balls onto a prepared sheet and refrigerate until chilled, about 30 minutes and up to 4 days.

4. Heat oven to 350°F. Lightly toss the chilled cookie dough balls in confectioners' sugar again and place onto the prepared sheets, spacing them 2 inches apart. Bake, rotating the positions of the baking sheets halfway through, until cookies are puffed, cracked and just set around edges, 9 to 11 minutes. Let cool on baking sheets for 3 minutes before transferring to a cooling rack to cool completely.

PER SERVING
About 70 calories, 3 g fat (2 g saturated fat), 1 g protein, 30 mg sodium, 10 g carbohydrates, 1 g fiber

Salted Chocolate Caramel Cookies

Perhaps the most decadent recipe in this book, these double chocolate cookies are studded with morsels of rich bittersweet chocolate and stuffed with melt-in-your-mouth caramels.

Active Time 1 hour 20 minutes | **Total Time** 2 hours 15 minutes | **Makes** 36

2	cups all-purpose flour
1⅓	cups unsweetened cocoa powder
2	teaspoons baking soda
¼	teaspoon salt
1	cup (2 sticks) unsalted butter, at room temperature
½	cup granulated sugar
1½	cups packed light brown sugar
2	large eggs, at room temperature
2	teaspoons pure vanilla extract
¼	cup buttermilk
12	ounces bittersweet chocolate, chopped (about 2 cups)
36	soft caramels
	Flaky sea salt

1. Line a baking sheet with parchment paper. In a medium bowl, sift together flour, cocoa powder, baking soda and salt, then whisk to combine; set aside.

2. Using an electric mixer, beat butter and sugars in a large bowl on medium speed until light and fluffy, about 3 minutes. Reduce speed to low and add eggs one at a time, then vanilla.

3. Add flour mixture in two parts, alternating with buttermilk and beating until just incorporated. Fold in chocolate chunks by hand and then refrigerate for at least 30 minutes.

4. Shape dough into balls (about 2 tablespoons each). Place balls onto the prepared sheet and refrigerate while preparing caramels. With the back of a spoon, flatten each caramel into a ¾-inch-wide disk. Then flatten each dough ball into a disk and wrap around a flattened caramel; return to the baking sheet and refrigerate.

5. Heat oven to 350°F. Line 2 baking sheets with parchment paper. Place chilled dough onto the prepared sheets, spacing them 2 inches apart. Sprinkle with sea salt and bake, rotating the positions of the baking sheets halfway through, until set around edges, 10 to 12 minutes. Let cool on baking sheets for 5 minutes before transferring to a cooling rack to cool completely.

PER SERVING
About 225 calories, 11 g fat (6 g saturated fat), 3 g protein, 130 mg sodium, 31 g carbohydrates, 2 g fiber

Chapter 3

Slice & Bake Cookies

There's no better feeling than knowing there's dough in the fridge or freezer, just waiting to be sliced, baked and enjoyed. While the method to make the dough and bake the cookies stays the same throughout the chapter, the recipes couldn't be more different from one another — so whether you're craving something citrusy, chocolatey, fruity or even savory, you're covered.

WHITE CHOCOLATE RASPBERRY THINS 94

←

Chocolate-Pistachio Slice & Bakes

Trimmed with pistachios, these convenient cookies are super easy and sophisticated too. Who needs a tube of store-bought dough to satisfy a cookie craving? Not you!

Active Time 20 minutes | **Total Time** 30 minutes, plus chilling | **Makes** 40

1 cup all-purpose flour

½ cup unsweetened cocoa

¼ teaspoon baking soda

¼ teaspoon kosher salt

½ cup (1 stick) unsalted butter, at room temperature

½ cup sugar

2 teaspoons pure vanilla extract

1 large egg

½ cup shelled unsalted pistachios, chopped

1. In a medium bowl, whisk together flour, cocoa, baking soda and salt; set aside.

2. Using an electric mixer, beat butter and sugar on medium speed until light and fluffy, about 3 minutes. Reduce speed to low and beat in vanilla and egg to combine. Add flour mixture, beating until just incorporated.

3. Divide dough in half. Using a piece of plastic wrap to guide, roll the dough into 2 logs, each about 8 inches long and 1½ inches in diameter. Roll the logs in pistachios to coat evenly, then wrap each in a piece of plastic wrap. Refrigerate until firm, at least 1 hour.

4. Heat oven to 350°F. Line 2 baking sheets with parchment paper. Slice dough crosswise into ¼-inch-thick rounds; transfer to the baking sheets, spacing them 2 inches apart.

5. Bake until tops feel sandy to the touch, 11 to 13 minutes. Let cool on baking sheets for 2 minutes before transferring to a cooling rack to cool completely.

PER SERVING
About 55 calories, 3 g fat (1.5 g saturated fat), 1 g protein, 20 mg sodium, 6 g carbohydrates, 1 g fiber

Switch It Up!

Not a fan of pistachios? Roll this dough in any chopped nuts, such as **walnuts**, or **crushed hard candy**. (Pro tip: **Crushed peppermint candies** are great around the winter holidays!)

GIFT IT!
Stack cookies in cello bags,
tie with ribbon and then hand-deliver
to friends and family.

Matcha Cookies

Ground Japanese green tea adds an earthy pop to baked goods and drinks. Here, matcha lends its distinct flavor and gorgeous green hue to dainty shortbread biscuits.

Active Time 25 minutes | **Total Time** 35 minutes, plus chilling | **Makes** 24

- 1 cup all-purpose flour
- 1 tablespoon matcha green tea powder
- 1/4 teaspoon kosher salt
- 1/2 cup (1 stick) unsalted butter, at room temperature
- 1/4 cup sugar
- Melted semisweet and white chocolate, for dipping, optional

— INGREDIENT —
SPOTLIGHT
Matcha

Unlike other forms of green tea, this Japanese green tea doesn't get steeped in water but rather is added directly to lattes, smoothies, hot milk and sweet treats. Always look for culinary matcha when baking; ceremonial grade is better for drinking.

1. In a medium bowl, sift together flour, green tea powder and salt; set aside.

2. Using an electric mixer, beat butter and sugar in a large bowl on low speed until combined and smooth, about 3 minutes. Add flour mixture and mix until dough comes together.

3. Divide dough in half, place each half on a piece of plastic wrap and shape both into 1 1/2-inch-thick logs. Wrap in plastic wrap and refrigerate for at least 30 minutes and up to a week.

4. Heat oven to 350°F. Line 2 baking sheets with parchment paper. Slice dough crosswise into 1/4-inch-thick rounds; transfer to the baking sheets, spacing them 2 inches apart.

5. Bake, rotating the positions of the baking sheets halfway through, until dough no longer looks raw and cookies are just barely set at edges, 8 to 9 minutes. Let cool completely on baking sheets on a cooling rack.

6. Once cool, dip half of each cookie into melted chocolate if desired, and let set.

PER SERVING
About 60 calories, 4 g fat (2.5 g saturated fat), 1 g protein, 20 mg sodium, 6 g carbohydrates, 0 g fiber

**TEST
KITCHEN
TIP**

To melt chocolate, place
chopped pieces in a bowl and
microwave at 50 percent power,
stirring at 30-second intervals.
Chocolate will still hold its shape
when partially melted,
so be careful not
to overheat.

White Chocolate Raspberry Thins

Freeze-dried raspberries are the secret to this cookie's beautiful pink hue and subtly fruity flavor. (See photo, page 88.)

Active Time 25 minutes | **Total Time** 40 minutes, plus chilling and cooling | **Makes** 24 to 48

2 1/2   cups freeze-dried raspberries, plus more for serving

2 1/2   cups all-purpose flour

1/2   teaspoon baking powder

1/4   teaspoon kosher salt

1   cup (2 sticks) unsalted butter, at room temperature

3/4   cup sugar

1   large egg

1 1/2   teaspoons pure vanilla extract

White chocolate, melted, for serving

1. In a food processor, finely grind freeze-dried raspberries (you should have a scant 1/2 cup). In a large bowl, whisk together raspberry powder, flour, baking powder and salt; set aside.

2. Using an electric mixer, beat butter and sugar in another large bowl on medium speed until light and fluffy, 3 minutes. Beat in egg and then vanilla. Reduce speed to low and gradually add in flour mixture, mixing until just incorporated.

3. Shape dough into 2 logs. Using your hands or 2 clean rulers on the sides, press each log into two 2-inch-long squared-off logs. Wrap in plastic wrap and freeze for 20 minutes.

4. Heat oven to 350°F. Line 2 baking sheets with parchment paper. Slice dough crosswise into 1/8-inch-thick squares; transfer to the baking sheets, spacing them 2 inches apart.

5. Bake, rotating the positions of the baking sheets halfway through, until cookies are light golden brown around edges, 10 to 12 minutes. Let cool on baking sheets for 5 minutes before transferring to a cooling rack to cool completely.

6. Once cool, drizzle with melted white chocolate and sprinkle with crushed freeze-dried raspberries.

PER SERVING
About 90 calories, 5 g fat (3 g saturated fat), 1 g protein, 20 mg sodium, 10 g carbohydrates, 1 g fiber

---

Bonus Recipe!

No-Bake Strawberry-Chocolate Clusters

Microwave **8 ounces bittersweet chocolate chips** in 30-second increments, stirring in between, until melted and smooth. Drop 15 teaspoonfuls melted chocolate onto a parchment-lined baking sheet. Top each with **3 freeze-dried strawberries.** Drop another spoonful chocolate onto each strawberry stack, letting chocolate drip down slightly. Sprinkle with **crushed freeze-dried strawberries** and refrigerate until set, 10 minutes.

Lemon-Thyme Coins

Though usually associated with savory dishes, fresh herbs like thyme can really bring your baked goods to the next level.

Active Time 25 minutes | **Total Time** 40 minutes, plus chilling and cooling
Makes 24 to 48

2 ¾ cups all-purpose flour
 ½ teaspoon baking powder
 ¼ teaspoon kosher salt
  1 cup (2 sticks) unsalted butter, at room temperature
 ¾ cup granulated sugar
  1 tablespoon fresh thyme leaves, plus more for serving, optional
  4 teaspoons finely grated lemon zest
  1 large egg
1 ½ teaspoons pure vanilla extract
  2 cups confectioners' sugar
 ¼ cup fresh lemon juice

1. In a large bowl, whisk together flour, baking powder and salt; set aside. Using an electric mixer, beat butter and sugar in another large bowl on medium speed until light and fluffy, about 3 minutes. Add thyme and 2 teaspoons lemon zest. Beat in egg, then vanilla. Reduce speed to low and gradually add flour mixture, mixing until just incorporated.

2. Shape dough into two 1½-inch-diameter logs. Wrap in plastic wrap and freeze for 20 minutes.

3. Heat oven to 350°F. Line 2 baking sheets with parchment paper. Slice dough crosswise into ⅛-inch-thick rounds; transfer to the baking sheets, spacing them 2 inches apart.

4. Bake, rotating the positions of the baking sheets halfway through, until light golden brown around edges, 10 to 12 minutes, Let cool on baking sheets for 5 minutes before transferring to a cooling rack to cool completely.

5. In a bowl, combine confectioners' sugar, lemon juice and remaining 2 teaspoons lemon zest. Spoon over cooled cookies. Sprinkle with additional thyme if desired.

PER SERVING
About 95 calories, 4 g fat (3 g saturated fat), 1 g protein, 20 mg sodium, 14 g carbohydrates, 0 g fiber

Pecan Crescent Cookies

While the original recipe for this cookie can be traced back to 7th-century Arabia, many countries have their own versions made with the same basic ingredients: Mexican wedding cookies, Russian tea cakes, Viennese crescents and snowballs, to name a few.

Active Time 40 minutes | **Total Time** 55 minutes, plus chilling | **Makes** 50

1   cup pecans (about 3 ounces)

1   cup confectioners' sugar

1   cup (2 sticks) unsalted butter, cut into small pieces

1   teaspoon pure vanilla extract

2   cups all-purpose flour

1/4   teaspoon kosher salt

1/8   teaspoon ground cinnamon

Switch It Up!

Walnut Crescent Cookies

Swap in **1 cup walnuts** and **3/4 teaspoon ground cardamom** for the pecans in Step 1. Freeze crescents for 20 minutes before baking in Step 4.

1. In a food processor, pulse pecans and 3/4 cup confectioners' sugar until pecans are finely ground. Add butter and process until smooth. Mix in vanilla. Add flour and salt, and pulse to combine.

2. Shape dough into 1-inch-diameter logs, wrap in plastic wrap and refrigerate until firm, at least 1 1/2 hours.

3. Heat oven to 350°F. Line 2 baking sheets with parchment paper. Cut off a 1/4-inch-thick slice of dough (about 1 1/2 teaspoons) and roll into a 3 1/2-inch log with tapered ends, then bend into a crescent shape and place onto a prepared baking sheet. Repeat with remaining dough.

4. Bake, rotating the positions of the baking sheets halfway through, until cookies are set and just barely turning golden brown around edges, 15 to 18 minutes. Let cool completely on the baking sheets.

5. In a small bowl, combine cinnamon and remaining 1/4 cup confectioners' sugar. Liberally dust cookies with cinnamon-sugar mixture before serving.

PER SERVING

About 75 calories, 5 g fat (2.5 g saturated fat), 1 g protein, 10 mg sodium, 7 g carbohydrates, 0 g fiber

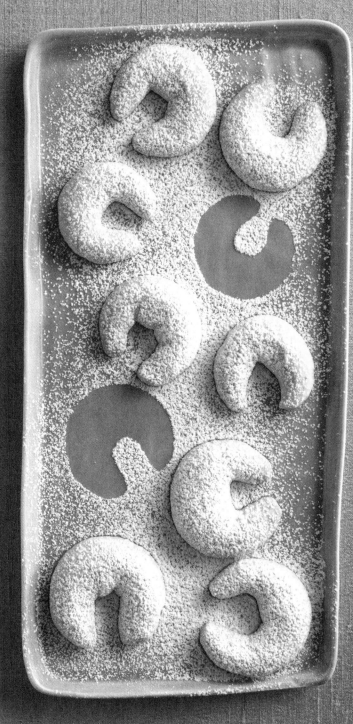

Chocolate-Citrus Cran Wheels

These chocolate-citrus wheels are the cookie adaptation of the chocolate-dipped fruit slices you find at specialty stores and bakeries.

Active Time 40 minutes | **Total Time** 1 hour 15 minutes, plus chilling and cooling | **Makes** 48

2 cups all-purpose flour

¼ teaspoon baking soda

¼ teaspoon kosher salt

¾ cup dried cranberries

½ cup confectioners' sugar

½ cup granulated sugar

¾ cup (1 ½ sticks) unsalted butter, at room temperature

1 teaspoon orange zest

1 teaspoon pure vanilla extract

¼ teaspoon ground cinnamon

Melted white or dark chocolate (about 12 ounces), for dipping

Dried orange slices, optional

Switch It Up!

Lemon-Apricot

Replace cranberries with **¾ cup coarsely chopped dried apricots**. Use **lemon zest** instead of orange.

Cherry-Almond

Replace cranberries with **¾ cup dried cherries**. Add **½ teaspoon pure almond extract** along with **vanilla**.

1. In a medium bowl, whisk together flour, baking soda and salt; set aside.

2. In a food processor, pulse dried cranberries, confectioners' sugar and granulated sugar until cranberries are very finely chopped; transfer to a large mixing bowl.

3. Using an electric mixer, beat cranberry mixture and butter in a large bowl on medium-high speed until combined, about 1 to 2 minutes. Beat in orange zest, vanilla and cinnamon. Reduce speed to low and gradually add flour mixture, mixing until just incorporated.

4. Divide dough in half. Roll each half into a 2-inch-diameter log; wrap tightly with plastic wrap. Refrigerate overnight or up to a week.

5. Heat oven to 350°F. Line a large baking sheet with parchment paper. Slice dough crosswise into ¼-inch-thick rounds; transfer to the baking sheet, spacing them about 1 inch apart.

6. Bake until golden brown around edges, 15 to 17 minutes. Let cool on baking sheet for 5 minutes before transferring to a cooling rack to cool completely. Repeat slicing and baking with the remaining dough.

7. Dip cooled cookies halfway into melted chocolate; decorate with orange slices if desired. Place onto a parchment-lined baking sheet. Refrigerate until set, at least 15 minutes. Cookies can be stored in airtight containers in the freezer for up to 2 weeks.

PER SERVING

About 100 calories, 5 g fat (4 g saturated fat), 1 g protein, 50 mg sodium, 14 g carbohydrates, 0 g fiber

Cinnamon-Roll Sugar Cookies

With a swirl of cinnamon goodness and a sinfully sweet icing, this dessert really delivers. Plus, baking a batch will make your kitchen smell beyond amazing.

Active Time 25 minutes | **Total Time** 1 hour | **Makes** 48

For the Cookies

2 3/4 cups all-purpose flour

1/2 teaspoon baking powder

1/2 teaspoon kosher salt

1 cup (2 sticks) unsalted butter, at room temperature

3/4 cup granulated sugar

1 large egg

1 1/2 teaspoons pure vanilla extract

For the Filling

1/4 cup packed light brown sugar

2 tablespoons granulated sugar

2 teaspoons ground cinnamon

For the Icing

1 cup confectioners' sugar

4 tablespoons whole milk

1. Prepare the cookies: In a large bowl, whisk together flour, baking powder and salt; set aside.

2. Using an electric mixer, beat butter and sugar in a large bowl on medium speed until light and fluffy, about 3 minutes. Beat in egg and then vanilla. Reduce speed to low and gradually add flour mixture, mixing until just incorporated.

3. Divide dough in half and shape into 2 disks; roll each disk between 2 sheets of lightly floured parchment paper into a 7- by 10-inch rectangle, 1/4 inch thick. Refrigerate until firm but pliable, about 10 minutes.

4. Heat oven to 350°F. Line 4 large baking sheets with parchment paper.

5. Prepare the filling: In a small bowl, combine sugars and ground cinnamon. Sprinkle rectangles with sugar mixture. Starting with one of the long ends facing you, tightly roll up 1 rectangle using the parchment paper to neatly guide the dough. (Press dough back together if it cracks.)

6. Working quickly, repeat with remaining rectangle. Return 1 roll of dough to the fridge. Slice other roll crosswise into 1/4-inch-thick slices; transfer to the baking sheets, spacing them at least 1 inch apart.

7. Bake, rotating the positions of the baking sheets halfway through, until light golden brown, 12 to 14 minutes. Let cool on baking sheets for 5 minutes before transferring to a cooling rack to cool completely. Repeat with remaining dough, letting it soften until pliable but still firm before slicing.

8. Meanwhile, prepare the icing: In a small bowl, combine confectioners' sugar with milk. Drizzle icing over cooled cookies.

PER SERVING

About 90 calories, 4 g fat (2 g saturated fat), 1 g protein, 30 mg sodium, 13 g carbohydrates, 0 g fiber

Lemon Icebox Cookies

Sometimes the simplest things are the best things. These citrusy cookies — made with just a few ingredients — are uncomplicated, uninvolved and unapologetically delicious.

Active Time 20 minutes | **Total Time** 1 hour 20 minutes, plus chilling and cooling | **Makes** 96

1 2/3 cups all-purpose flour

1 teaspoon baking powder

1/4 teaspoon baking soda

1/4 teaspoon kosher salt

1/2 cup (1 stick) unsalted butter, at room temperature

3/4 cup granulated sugar

1 large egg yolk

1 tablespoon lemon zest plus 2 tablespoons lemon juice, from about 3 lemons

---

Switch It Up!

Orange Icebox Cookies
Prepare as directed, but substitute
1 tablespoon freshly grated orange zest and
2 tablespoons fresh orange juice for the
lemon zest and juice.

1. In a medium bowl, whisk together flour, baking powder, baking soda and salt; set aside.

2. Using an electric mixer, beat butter and sugar in a large bowl on medium speed until light and fluffy, about 3 minutes. Beat in egg yolk, lemon zest and lemon juice until combined. Reduce speed to low and beat in flour mixture until just blended.

3. Divide dough in half. On parchment paper, form dough into two 12-inch logs. Wrap the logs and refrigerate overnight or freeze until very firm, at least 2 hours.

4. Heat oven to 375°F. Line 2 large baking sheets with parchment paper. Slice 1 log crosswise into ¼-inch-thick rounds; transfer to the baking sheets, spacing them 1 inch apart.

5. Bake, rotating the positions of the baking sheets halfway through, until set and golden brown around edges, 10 to 12 minutes. Transfer cookies to a cooling rack to cool completely. Repeat with remaining dough.

PER SERVING
About 25 calories, 1 g fat (1 g saturated fat), 0 g protein, 20 mg sodium, 3 g carbohydrates, 0 g fiber

Chocolate & Sea Salt Shortbread Cookies

The same buttery shortbread is the canvas for these three cookies. Shaping the dough into a log and chilling in the fridge only makes for better cookies — it not only helps to solidify the butter and firm up the dough but also allows for the flavors to concentrate (read: become more delicious).

Active Time 35 minutes | **Total Time** 1 hour 5 minutes, plus chilling and cooling | **Makes** 36

2 cups all-purpose flour

1/4 teaspoon baking powder

1/2 teaspoon kosher salt

1 cup (2 sticks) unsalted butter, at room temperature

3/4 cup confectioners' sugar

2 teaspoons pure vanilla extract

12 ounces bittersweet chocolate, chopped

Flaky sea salt, for garnish

Switch It Up!

Fruit & Nut

Omit chocolate and sea salt, and stir in **1/2 cup chopped toasted nuts** and **1/2 cup chopped dried fruit** at the end of Step 2.

Lemon

Omit chocolate and sea salt, and stir in **1 1/2 tablespoons lemon zest** at the end of Step 2. Roll dough into logs and then roll logs in **1/2 cup yellow sanding sugar** before slicing, coating edges.

1. In a large bowl, whisk together flour, baking powder and salt; set aside.

2. Using an electric mixer, beat butter and confectioners' sugar in another large bowl on medium speed until light and fluffy, 1 to 2 minutes. Beat in vanilla. Reduce speed to low and gradually add in flour mixture until combined. Stir 4 ounces chocolate into dough.

3. Divide dough in half and shape each half into a log about 7 1/2 inches long and 1 3/4 inches in diameter. Wrap tightly in plastic wrap and chill for at least 4 hours or up to overnight.

4. Heat oven to 350°F. Line 2 baking sheets with parchment paper. Slice each log into 1/4-inch-thick rounds; transfer to the baking sheets, placing them 1 inch apart.

5. Bake, rotating the positions of the baking sheets halfway through, until edges are lightly golden brown, 12 to 15 minutes. Transfer to a cooling rack to cool completely.

6. Line a baking sheet with parchment paper. Microwave remaining 8 ounces chocolate in a bowl for 30 seconds; stir. Continue to microwave and stir in 10-second intervals until melted. Dip half of each cookie into melted chocolate and place onto the prepared sheet. Sprinkle lightly with sea salt. Refrigerate until chocolate is set, 10 to 15 minutes.

PER SERVING

About 130 calories, 9 g fat (6 g saturated fat), 1 g protein, 160 mg sodium, 12 g carbohydrates, 1 g fiber

Fruit & Nut

Lemon

Chocolate &
Sea Salt

GIFT IT!
A cookie tin lined with tissue paper
allows ample room for a sweet sampling.

Lime & Coconut Coins

For a bright and citrusy bite-sized cookie, look no further than this easy option that is topped off with a sweet glaze and a sprinkle of toasted coconut.

Active Time 35 minutes | **Total Time** 50 minutes, plus chilling and cooling | **Makes** 120

2 ³/₄ cups all-purpose flour

¹/₂ teaspoon baking powder

¹/₄ teaspoon kosher salt

1 cup (2 sticks) unsalted butter, at room temperature

³/₄ cup granulated sugar

1 large egg

1 ¹/₂ teaspoons pure vanilla extract

2 cups confectioners' sugar

¹/₄ cup fresh lime juice

2 teaspoons grated lime zest

Toasted coconut, for serving

TEST KITCHEN TIP

For how to toast coconut, see page 163.

1. In a large bowl, whisk together flour, baking powder and salt; set aside.

2. Using an electric mixer, beat butter and sugar in a large bowl on medium speed until light and fluffy, about 3 minutes. Beat in egg and then vanilla. Reduce speed to low and gradually add flour mixture, mixing until just incorporated. Shape dough into 2 logs, each 1¹/₂ inches in diameter. Wrap in plastic wrap and freeze for 20 minutes.

3. Heat oven to 350°F. Line 2 baking sheets with parchment paper. Slice dough crosswise into ¹/₈-inch-thick rounds; transfer to the baking sheets, spacing them 1 inch apart.

4. Bake, rotating the positions of the baking sheets halfway through, until cookies are lightly golden brown around edges, 10 to 12 minutes. Let cool on baking sheets for 5 minutes before transferring to a cooling rack to cool completely.

5. In a small bowl, whisk together confectioners' sugar, lime juice and lime zest. Spoon glaze over each cookie, then sprinkle with toasted coconut and let set.

PER SERVING

About 35 calories, 2 g fat (1 g saturated fat), 0 g protein, 10 mg sodium, 5 g carbohydrates, 0 g fiber

Cookie Cheat!

No time to bake? Pick up a box of **vanilla wafer cookies**, then dress them up with this quick homemade glaze and a sprinkle of **toasted coconut**. (Just follow Step 5 of this recipe.)

Cranberry Shortbread

Thanks to tart cranberries, bright orange zest and fresh rosemary, these sophisticated shortbreads are perfect for anyone looking for a well-balanced cookie.

Active Time 20 minutes | **Total Time** 1 hour 20 minutes | **Makes** 28

⅓ cup sugar

¼ teaspoon chopped fresh rosemary

⅓ cup frozen cranberries (about 1½ ounces)

¾ cup (1½ sticks) unsalted butter, at room temperature

½ teaspoon pure vanilla extract

1 teaspoon finely grated orange zest

1½ cups all-purpose flour

¼ teaspoon kosher salt

≡ INGREDIENT ≡
SPOTLIGHT
Frozen Cranberries

Available year-round, frozen cranberries may work better than fresh (yes, really!) in some baked goods. You can easily and cleanly chop them into pea-size pieces in a food processor. Plus, they'll thaw as you add them to the dough, so you'll have little bursts of tartness.

1. Line 2 baking sheets with parchment paper. In a food processor, pulse sugar and rosemary until very finely chopped. Transfer to a large bowl. Wipe out the bowl of the processor, add frozen cranberries and pulse to break up into pea-size pieces.

2. Using an electric mixer, beat butter and rosemary sugar on medium speed until very well combined, 1 to 2 minutes. Beat in vanilla and zest.

3. Reduce speed to low and gradually add flour and salt, mixing until just incorporated. Add chopped cranberries and mix to combine. Dough should look streaky with bits of cranberries.

4. On a piece of plastic wrap, form dough into a 7½- by 2¾- by 1-inch-thick rectangle. Chill dough until firm, about 45 minutes in the freezer or 2 hours in the fridge.

5. Heat oven to 325°F. Slice dough crosswise into ¼-inch-thick rectangles; transfer to the baking sheets, spacing them 2 inches apart. Bake, rotating the positions of the baking sheets halway through, until light golden brown around edges, 15 to 18 minutes. Let cool completely on the baking sheets.

PER SERVING
About 80 calories, 5 g fat (3 g saturated fat), 1 g protein, 20 mg sodium, 8 g carbohydrates, 0 g fiber

Nutty Shortbread

This cookie's buttery, crumbly texture comes from being made with nuts, not flour.

Active Time 20 minutes | **Total Time** 35 minutes, plus chilling | **Makes** 18

- ½ cup (1 stick) unsalted butter, at room temperature
- ½ cup granulated sugar
- 1 teaspoon alcohol-free pure vanilla extract
- 1½ cups almond flour
- ½ cup ground hazelnuts
  Pinch sea salt

1. Using an electric mixer, beat together butter, sugar and vanilla in a medium bowl on medium speed until well blended, about 2 minutes.

2. Stir in almond flour, ground hazelnuts and salt until a firm dough forms.

3. Roll dough into a 2-inch log and wrap in plastic wrap. Refrigerate until firm, at least 30 minutes.

4. Heat oven to 350°F. Line a baking sheet with parchment paper. Slice dough into 18 rounds; transfer to the baking sheet, spacing them 2 inches apart.

5. Bake until firm and light golden brown, about 10 minutes. Let cool on baking sheet for 5 minutes before transferring to a cooling rack to cool completely.

PER SERVING
About 135 calories, 11 g fat (4 g saturated fat), 2 g protein, 10 mg sodium, 8 g carbohydrates, 1 g fiber

Earl Grey Tea Cookies

Infuse cookies with a dash of tea to add flecks of color and a subtle delicate flavor. Made with Earl Grey tea leaves, these cookies are perfect with a piping-hot afternoon cup.

Active Time 10 minutes | **Total Time** 45 minutes, plus chilling and cooling | **Makes** 48

2 3/4 cups all-purpose flour

2 tablespoons fine Earl Grey tea leaves

1/2 teaspoon baking powder

1/4 teaspoon kosher salt

1 cup (2 sticks) unsalted butter, at room temperature

3/4 cup granulated sugar

1 large egg

1 teaspoon grated orange zest

≈ **INGREDIENT SPOTLIGHT** ≈

Earl Grey Tea

Citrusy and bright, this quintessentially British brew is a blend of bergamot extract and black tea. Buy loose leaves or cut open a traditional tea bag (such as Twinings).

1. In a large bowl, whisk together flour, tea leaves, baking powder and salt; set aside.

2. In a food processor, process butter and sugar until smooth. Add egg and zest, and pulse to combine. Then add flour mixture and pulse to combine.

3. Transfer dough to a lightly floured surface and roll into 2 logs, about 2 inches in diameter. Wrap each in plastic wrap and chill for at least 30 minutes.

4. Heat oven to 350°F. Line 2 large baking sheets with parchment paper. Slice the logs crosswise into 1/8-inch-thick rounds; transfer to the baking sheets, spacing them 1 inch apart.

5. Bake, rotating the positions of the baking sheets halfway through, until light golden brown around edges, 14 to 16 minutes. Let cool on baking sheets for 5 minutes before transferring to a cooling rack to cool completely.

PER SERVING

About 70 calories, 4 g fat (2.5 g saturated fat), 1 g protein, 20 mg sodium, 8 g carbohydrates, 0 g fiber

GIFT IT!
For a hostess present that does double duty, pile cookies high in a brand-new pretty dish. Then wrap with cellophane and tie closed with a ribbon.

Cranberry-Orange Spice Cookies

These fresh, fruity cookies are studded with chopped crystallized ginger and dried cranberries.

Active Time 20 minutes | **Total Time** 1 hour, plus chilling and cooling | **Makes** 60

2 ¾ cups all-purpose flour

¼ teaspoon baking soda

¼ teaspoon kosher salt

1 cup (2 sticks) unsalted butter, at room temperature

¾ cup granulated sugar

1 large egg

1 teaspoon pure vanilla extract

½ cup dried cranberries, finely chopped

¼ cup crystallized ginger, finely chopped

2 teaspoons orange zest

1 teaspoon pumpkin pie spice

3 tablespoons green sanding sugar

3 tablespoons red sanding sugar

TEST KITCHEN TIP

Press each side of the log into fun-colored sanding sugars to coat.

1. In a medium bowl, combine flour, baking soda and salt; set aside.

2. Using an electric mixer, beat butter and sugar in a large bowl on medium speed until light and fluffy, about 3 minutes. Add egg and vanilla, and beat until well mixed. Reduce speed to low and gradually beat in flour mixture until just blended, occasionally scraping the side of the bowl. Stir in cranberries, ginger, orange zest and pumpkin pie spice until well mixed.

3. Divide dough in half. On a lightly floured surface, shape each half into a 10-inch log. Using your hands or 2 clean rulers on the sides, press each log into a 10-inch squared-off log. Wrap each in plastic wrap and chill until firm enough to slice, 2 hours in the freezer or overnight in the refrigerator. (Logs can be frozen for up to a month.)

4. Heat oven to 350°F. Line 2 baking sheets with parchment paper. On another sheet of parchment paper, place green sugar. Unwrap 1 log and press sides into sugar to coat. Slice the log crosswise into ¼-inch-thick squares; transfer to the baking sheets, placing them 1 inch apart. Bake until golden brown, 14 to 16 minutes. Transfer cookies to a cooling rack to cool completely. Repeat with red sugar and the second log. Store cookies in a tightly sealed container at room temperature for up to a week or in the freezer for up to 3 months.

PER SERVING
About 70 calories, 3 g fat (2 g saturated fat), 1 g protein, 50 mg sodium, 9 g carbohydrates, 0 g fiber

Chocolate Pinwheels

Achieving the swirl is a cinch: Just stack one dough on top of another, roll tightly, chill and slice.

Active Time 30 minutes | **Total Time** 1 hour, plus chilling and cooling | **Makes** 48

2 ¾ cups plus 2 tablespoons all-purpose flour

¼ teaspoon baking soda

¼ teaspoon kosher salt

1 cup (2 sticks) unsalted butter, at room temperature

¾ cup granulated sugar

1 large egg

1 teaspoon pure vanilla extract

⅓ cup miniature semisweet chocolate chips

¼ cup confectioners' sugar

1 ounce unsweetened chocolate, melted

1 tablespoon cocoa powder

1. In a medium bowl, whisk together 2¾ cups flour, baking soda and salt; set aside.

2. Using an electric mixer, beat butter and sugar in a large bowl on medium-high speed until smooth and creamy, about 1 minute. Beat in egg and vanilla. Reduce speed to low and gradually add in flour mixture until just combined.

3. Remove half the dough from the mixing bowl. Stir in chocolate chips, confectioners' sugar, melted chocolate and cocoa powder. Stir remaining 2 tablespoons flour into the other half of dough.

4. On a piece of parchment paper, roll plain dough into a 10- by 14-inch rectangle. Repeat with chocolate dough. Lift the plain rectangle, still on the parchment paper, and place it, dough side down, on top of the chocolate rectangle so that the edges line up evenly. Peel off the top sheet of parchment paper. Starting from the long side, tightly roll rectangles together, jelly-roll fashion, to form a log. Cut the log in half crosswise. Wrap each half in plastic wrap and freeze for 2 hours or refrigerate overnight.

5. Heat oven to 375°F. Line 2 baking sheets with parchment paper. Using a sharp knife, slice 1 log crosswise into ¼-inch-thick rounds; transfer to the baking sheet, spacing them 2 inches apart.

6. Bake until edges are golden brown, 10 to 12 minutes. Transfer to a cooling rack to cool completely. Repeat with remaining dough. Store cookies in airtight containers at room temperature for up to a week or in the freezer for up to 3 months.

PER SERVING

About 90 calories, 5 g fat (3 g saturated fat), 1 g protein, 60 mg sodium, 10 g carbohydrates, 0 g fiber

---

Switch It Up!

PB&J Pinwheels

In Step 2, beat **⅓ cup creamy peanut butter** in with the butter and sugar. After dividing the dough in half, add **½ teaspoon raspberry extract** and **red food coloring** to one half of the dough, beating until well incorporated. Use a rubber spatula to stir **⅓ cup creamy peanut butter** into the other half of the dough.

Chapter 4

Bars, Blondies & Brownies

These sweet treats are a cinch to pull off — no rolling, shaping or chilling required! Simply whip up a batch of dough, spread it in a pan, bake, cool and cut. Or, take your baking to the next level with homemade sauces, crunchy toppings and more.

AVOCADO BROWNIES 142

←

Shortbread Bars

The same buttery base forms the crust for this trio of layered treats. Bake the base layer first, then choose how to top it — or try out all three variations!

Active Time 10 minutes | **Total Time** 40 minutes | **Makes** 24

Shortbread Dough

1 1/2 cups (2 1/2 sticks) unsalted butter, at room temperature

3/4 cup granulated sugar

1 teaspoon pure vanilla extract

3 cups all-purpose flour

1/2 teaspoon kosher salt

1. Heat oven to 350°F. Line a 9- by 13-inch baking pan with parchment paper, leaving a 2-inch overhang on the two long sides.

2. Using an electric mixer, beat butter and sugar in a large bowl on medium speed until combined, 2 minutes. Beat in vanilla.

3. Reduce speed to low and gradually add flour and salt, mixing until just incorporated. Press or spread mixture into the bottom of the prepared pan. Bake until light golden brown, 25 to 30 minutes. Let cool, then top as desired (see ideas, at right).

1

Chocolate–Peppermint Bars

Active Time 20 minutes
Total Time 55 minutes, plus chilling
Makes 24

1. Prepare **Shortbread Dough** as directed.

2. Using an electric mixer, beat **6 tablespoons unsalted butter** (at room temperature) in a large bowl on medium speed until smooth, 3 minutes. Reduce speed to low and gradually add **3 cups confectioners' sugar** until fully incorporated. Add **3 tablespoons heavy cream** and **1 1/2 teaspoons pure peppermint extract** and beat for 2 minutes. Spread over cooled crust and refrigerate until firm, at least 30 minutes.

3. In a medium bowl, melt **12 ounces semisweet chocolate chips** and **6 tablespoons unsalted butter** (cut into pieces) in microwave on 50 percent power in 30-second intervals, stirring after each interval, until melted and smooth. Spread onto peppermint layer and refrigerate until set, at least 30 minutes, before cutting into pieces.

PER SERVING
About 370 calories,
22.5 g fat (14 g saturated fat),
2 g protein, 45 mg sodium,
42 g carbohydrates, 1 g fiber

2

Citrus Crumble Bars

Active Time 15 minutes
Total Time 55 minutes
Makes 24

1. Prepare **Shortbread Dough** as directed, but transfer 3/4 cup dough to a piece of plastic wrap, roll into a log and freeze until firm, 30 minutes.

2. Spread remaining dough into the pan and bake only 12 minutes; let cool completely.

3. In a small bowl, combine **1 cup red currant jam** with **2 tablespoons Grand Marnier** or other orange liqueur and **1 teaspoon finely grated orange zest,** and spread over dough.

4. Using a box grater, coarsely grate frozen dough over top. Bake until golden brown, 35 to 40 minutes. Let cool before cutting into pieces.

PER SERVING
About 200 calories,
11.5 g fat (7 g saturated fat),
2 g protein, 40 mg sodium,
23 g carbohydrates, 0 g fiber

3

Toffee-Pecan Bars

Active Time 15 minutes
Total Time 55 minutes
Makes 24

1. Prepare **Shortbread Dough** as directed.

2. In a heavy-bottomed medium saucepan, combine **2 cups granulated sugar** and **1/3 cup water.** Heat on medium (do not stir), swirling the pan occasionally, until sugar has dissolved.

3. Increase heat and boil until sugar is a deep caramel color (do not stir). Immediately remove from heat and stir in **3/4 cup heavy cream** (it will bubble up), then fold in **4 cups toasted pecans,** very roughly chopped.

4. Pour mixture over cooled crust and sprinkle with **flaky sea salt.** Let cool before cutting into pieces.

PER SERVING
About 375 calories,
25 g fat (8.5 g saturated fat),
3 g protein, 55 mg sodium,
38 g carbohydrates, 2 g fiber

Magic Bars

Also known as Hello Dolly Bars, these rich sweets are topped with caramel, chocolate, toffee, pretzel pieces and toasted coconut.

Active Time 15 minutes | **Total Time** 45 minutes, plus cooling and chilling | **Makes** 24

Nonstick cooking spray, for the pan

3/4 cup (1 1/2 sticks) unsalted butter, at room temperature

1/2 cup packed brown sugar

1/2 teaspoon kosher salt

1 large egg

1 1/2 teaspoons pure vanilla extract

2 cups all-purpose flour

3/4 cup caramel sauce

1/4 cup toffee bits

1/4 cup broken pretzels

1/2 cup toasted coconut

4 ounces melted bittersweet chocolate

1. Heat oven to 375°F. Lightly coat a 9- by 13-inch metal baking pan with nonstick cooking spray. Line with parchment paper, leaving a 2-inch overhang on the two long sides; spray paper.

2. Using an electric mixer, beat butter, brown sugar and salt in a large bowl on medium-high speed until creamy, 2 minutes. Beat in egg and vanilla. Reduce speed to low and beat in flour until just combined. Transfer batter to the prepared pan. With lightly floured hands, spread into even layer.

3. Bake until deep golden brown around edges, 25 to 30 minutes. Use overhangs to transfer to a cooling rack to cool completely.

4. Spread caramel sauce onto bars. Top with toffee bits, broken pretzels and toasted coconut. Drizzle with melted chocolate. Refrigerate until set, about 1 1/2 hours. Cut into 2-inch squares.

PER SERVING

About 180 calories, 10 g fat (6 g saturated fat), 2 g protein, 105 mg sodium, 24 g carbohydrates, 1 g fiber

Switch It Up!

Brown Sugar & Hazelnut Bars

In Step 4, spread **1/2 cup chocolate-hazelnut spread** onto bars. Sprinkle with **1 cup hazelnuts** (toasted, peeled and chopped), gently pressing to adhere. Use overhangs to transfer to a cutting board and cut into 1 1/2-inch squares.

Cherry-Ginger Hermit Bars

Spice cookies and bars date to medieval times, but *these* chewy confections are often associated with late 19th-century New England, when sailors would take tins of them on long voyages.

Active Time 20 minutes | **Total Time** 50 minutes, plus cooling | **Makes** 32

Nonstick cooking spray, for the pan

3 cups all-purpose flour

1 teaspoon baking soda

1 teaspoon cinnamon

½ teaspoon kosher salt

¾ cup (1 ½ sticks) unsalted butter, at room temperature

1 cup granulated sugar

½ cup molasses

½ cup dried cherries, chopped

⅓ cup candied ginger, chopped, plus sliced candied ginger, for serving

½ cup confectioners' sugar

1 teaspoon orange zest, plus more for serving

2 tablespoons fresh orange juice (from ½ small orange)

1. Heat oven to 350°F. Lightly coat a 9- by 13-inch metal baking pan with nonstick cooking spray. Line with parchment paper, leaving a 2-inch overhang on the two long sides; spray paper.

2. In a medium bowl, whisk together flour, baking soda, cinnamon and salt until combined; set aside.

3. Using an electric mixer, beat butter and sugar in a large bowl on high speed until light and fluffy, about 3 minutes. Add molasses and mix until fully incorporated. Reduce speed to low and gradually add flour mixture, beating until a soft dough forms. Fold in cherries and candied ginger.

4. Using your hands, press dough evenly into the prepared pan. Bake until puffed and just barely pulling away from sides, 25 to 30 minutes (it will keep cooking in the pan). Let cool completely in the pan.

5. In a medium bowl, whisk together confectioners' sugar, orange zest and juice until smooth. Drizzle glaze over cooled bars, then sprinkle with zest and sliced candied ginger if desired.

PER SERVING
About 140 calories, 4.5 g fat (2.5 g saturated fat), 1 g protein, 75 mg sodium, 24 g carbohydrates, 0 g fiber

Kitchen Sink Bars

Here's a delicious excuse to empty out all the odds and ends from your pantry! Experiment with whatever salty or sweet ingredients you have on hand — potato chips, cookie crumbs, you name it.

Active Time 20 minutes | **Total Time** 2 hours 55 minutes | **Makes** 16

Nonstick cooking spray, for the pan
3 1/2 cups pretzel twists
1/2 cup (1 stick) unsalted butter, melted
   Pinch kosher salt
   3 tablespoons packed dark brown sugar
   1 cup butterscotch chips
   1 cup semisweet chocolate chips
   1 cup packed shredded sweetened coconut
1/2 cup chopped roasted salted almonds
   1 14-ounce can sweetened condensed milk
   Flaky sea salt, optional

1. Heat oven to 350°F. Lightly coat a 9-inch square baking pan with nonstick cooking spray. Line with parchment paper, leaving a 2-inch overhang on two opposite sides; spray paper.

2. In a food processor, pulse pretzels until finely ground, 15 to 20 seconds; transfer to a medium bowl. Add butter, salt and brown sugar, and mix to combine. Press crust into the bottom of the prepared pan. Bake until dry to the touch and fragrant, 8 to 10 minutes.

3. Top crust with butterscotch and chocolate chips, coconut and almonds, pressing gently to compact. Top with condensed milk.

4. Bake until golden brown around edges, 25 to 30 minutes. Sprinkle with sea salt if desired. Let cool completely in the pan, about 2 hours. Use overhangs to transfer to a cutting board and cut into squares.

PER SERVING
About 390 calories, 20 g fat (12 g saturated fat), 6 g protein, 310 mg sodium, 48 g carbohydrates, 2 g fiber

Strawberry-Rhubarb Shortbread Bars

These cookies get their gorgeous color from food dye plus spring's finest seasonal fruits — strawberries and rhubarb. It works well with frozen rhubarb too, so you can make it all year round.

Active Time 30 minutes | **Total Time** 3 hours 30 minutes | **Makes** 16

1 1/2　cups sliced fresh or frozen rhubarb

　1　cup sliced fresh strawberries, plus more for garnish

　1/2　cup plus 1/3 cup granulated sugar

　1/4　cup water

　3　tablespoons confectioners' sugar

　1/2　teaspoon kosher salt

　1　cup plus 3 tablespoons all-purpose flour

　1/2　cup (1 stick) cold unsalted butter, cut into pieces

　2　large eggs plus 2 large egg yolks

　1　tablespoon fresh lemon zest

　5　drops red food coloring

≈ INGREDIENT ≈
SPOTLIGHT
Rhubarb

The stalks vary in hue, but it doesn't affect the flavor: Save your reddest stalks for recipes where color is important and use the paler stalks where it's not, such as in jam.

1. Heat oven to 350°F. Line a 9-inch square baking pan with parchment paper, leaving a 2-inch overhang on two opposite sides.

2. In a medium saucepan, combine rhubarb, strawberries, 1/2 cup granulated sugar and 1/4 cup water. Bring to a boil and cook until fruit is softened and beginning to break down, 2 to 4 minutes. Let cool completely.

3. Meanwhile, in a food processor, pulse confectioners' sugar, salt and 1 cup flour to combine, 4 to 5 times. Add butter and pulse until a coarse meal forms, 10 to 12 times. Press mixture firmly into the bottom of the prepared pan. Bake until golden brown around edges, 16 to 20 minutes. Let cool completely in the pan.

4. Wipe out the food processor, add rhubarb mixture and puree until very smooth, about 1 minute. Add eggs, egg yolks, zest and remaining 1/3 cup granulated sugar, and process until smooth, 15 to 20 seconds. Add food coloring and remaining 3 tablespoons flour, and pulse just until smooth. Pour over cooled crust.

5. Bake until set, 25 to 30 minutes. Let cool completely in the pan. Refrigerate for at least 2 hours or up to a day. When ready to serve, use overhangs to transfer to a cutting board and cut into squares. Garnish with sliced strawberries.

PER SERVING

About 155 calories, 7 g fat (4 g saturated fat), 2 g protein, 70 mg sodium, 21 g carbohydrates, 1 g fiber

Blueberry Crumb Bars

Bursting with blueberries, these streusel squares are an easier alternative to fresh-from-the-oven summer pies. No fussy pie crust, no rolling dough, no blind baking — just layers of buttery shortbread, fresh fruit and a crumbly sugar topping. Yum!

Active Time 20 minutes | **Total Time** 1 hour 30 minutes | **Makes** 18

Nonstick cooking spray, for the pan

2 1/2	cups all-purpose flour
3/4	cup granulated sugar
1	teaspoon ground cinnamon
1	teaspoon lemon zest plus 2 tablespoons juice
1/2	teaspoon kosher salt
1	cup (2 sticks) cold unsalted butter
2	teaspoons pure vanilla extract
4	cups fresh blueberries
1/2	cup packed brown sugar
2	tablespoons cornstarch

TEST
KITCHEN
TIP

For extra crunch, add
¼ **cup old-fashioned oats**
to the crumb mixture
before sprinkling
atop berries.

1. Heat oven to 375°F. Lightly coat a 9- by 13-inch baking pan with nonstick spray. Line with parchment paper, leaving a 2-inch overhang on the two long sides; spray paper.

2. In a food processor, pulse flour, granulated sugar, cinnamon, lemon zest and salt to combine, 4 to 5 times. Add butter and vanilla, and pulse until dough resembles crumbs, 10 to 12 times. Transfer half the dough to the prepared pan and firmly press into an even layer; bake for 15 minutes. Refrigerate remaining dough until ready to use.

3. In a large bowl, toss blueberries, brown sugar, cornstarch and lemon juice. Spread berry mixture over crust. Firmly squeeze chilled dough into small clumps and scatter over berries. Bake until topping is golden brown, 50 minutes to 1 hour. Use overhangs to transfer to a cooling rack to cool completely. Cut into squares. Bars can be made ahead, wrapped in plastic and refrigerated for up to a day.

PER SERVING

About 235 calories, 11 g fat (7 g saturated fat), 2 g protein, 140 mg sodium, 34 g carbohydrates, 1 g fiber

Grasshopper Bars

Grasshopper pie dates to the 1950s, when mousse-like chiffon pies were at the peak of their popularity. This bar variation is more family-friendly, subbing in green food coloring and peppermint extract for the traditional liqueur.

Active Time 25 minutes | **Total Time** 2 hours 25 minutes | **Makes** 20

For the Filling

- ½ cup milk
- 3 cups mini marshmallows
- 2 tablespoons (¼ stick) unsalted butter, cut into small pieces
- 1 cup plus 2 tablespoons heavy cream
- 2 teaspoons pure peppermint extract
- 1 teaspoon pure vanilla extract
  Green food coloring, optional

For the Crust

- 34 chocolate wafer cookies (such as Nabisco Famous Chocolate Wafers)
- 6 tablespoons (¾ stick) unsalted butter, melted

For the Topping

- ¾ cup heavy cream
- 6 ounces bittersweet chocolate, finely chopped

1. Prepare the filling: In a medium saucepan, heat milk on medium until hot. Add marshmallows and butter, and stir to melt. Remove from heat; stir in 2 tablespoons heavy cream, extracts and 6 to 8 drops food coloring (if using); let cool completely, about 1 hour.

2. Meanwhile, make the crust: Line a 9-inch square baking pan with parchment paper, leaving a 2-inch overhang on two opposite sides. In a food processor, pulse cookies to form fine crumbs, 8 to 12 times. Add butter and pulse to combine. Press crust evenly into the bottom of the prepared pan and refrigerate while the filling cools.

3. Once marshmallow filling is cool, using an electric mixer, beat remaining 1 cup cream in a medium bowl on high speed until stiff peaks form, about 6 to 8 minutes. Fold a spoonful of cream into marshmallow mixture to loosen, then fold in remaining cream and spread on top of chilled crust. Refrigerate until set, at least 30 minutes.

4. Make the topping: In a small pot, heat cream on medium until hot but not boiling. Remove from heat and add chocolate; let sit 1 minute, then stir until melted and smooth. Spread evenly over filling and refrigerate until set, at least 30 minutes or up to a day. When ready to serve, use overhangs to transfer to a cutting board and cut into 20 pieces.

PER SERVING
About 235 calories, 18 g fat (11 g saturated fat), 3 g protein, 95 mg sodium, 19 g carbohydrates, 1 g fiber

Millionaire Shortbread

This classic cookie hailing from Scotland and named for its rich flavor is the perfect trio of buttery shortbread, gooey caramel and rich chocolate. A sprinkling of flaky sea salt makes it even more divine.

Active Time 40 minutes | **Total Time** 3 hours 25 minutes | **Makes** 32

Nonstick cooking spray, for the pan

1/2 cup confectioners' sugar

1 1/4 cups (2 1/2 sticks) unsalted butter, at room temperature

1/2 cup slivered almonds, toasted and finely chopped

2 cups all-purpose flour

1 teaspoon kosher salt

1 14-ounce can sweetened condensed milk

1 cup packed dark brown sugar

1/2 cup pure honey

3/4 cup heavy cream

2 teaspoons pure vanilla extract

8 ounces bittersweet chocolate, chopped

Flaky sea salt, for sprinkling

1. Heat oven to 350°F. Lightly coat a 9- by 13-inch baking pan with nonstick cooking spray. Line pan with parchment paper, leaving a 2-inch overhang on the two long sides; spray paper.

2. Using an electric mixer, beat confectioners' sugar and 3/4 cup butter in a large bowl on medium speed until light and fluffy, 1 to 2 minutes. Reduce speed to low and beat in almonds, flour and 1/2 teaspoon kosher salt until just combined. Press dough into the bottom of the prepared pan. Bake until golden brown, 25 to 28 minutes. Let cool completely in the pan.

3. In a medium saucepan, combine condensed milk, brown sugar, honey, 1/2 cup cream and remaining 1/2 teaspoon kosher salt and 1/2 cup butter. Cook on medium, stirring constantly, until a candy thermometer reaches 236°F, 24 to 26 minutes. Remove from heat; stir in vanilla. Immediately pour caramel over shortbread. Let sit at room temperature until set, 1 to 1 1/2 hours.

4. In a bowl, microwave chocolate and remaining 1/4 cup cream for 30 seconds; stir. Continue to microwave in 10-second intervals, stirring after each until melted and smooth. Pour melted chocolate over caramel and spread with an offset spatula. Sprinkle with sea salt. Freeze until set, 15 to 20 minutes. When ready to serve, use overhangs to transfer to a cutting board and cut into squares. Store, refrigerated, in an airtight container for up to a week.

PER SERVING

About 250 calories, 14 g fat (9 g saturated fat), 3 g protein, 225 mg sodium, 30 g carbohydrates, 1 g fiber

PB&J Bars

Here's a little secret: This drool-worthy dessert starts with a can of chickpeas. Pulsing chickpeas, honey and vanilla in a food processor to create a cookie-dough-like batter gives these gluten-, egg- and cholesterol-free bars a dense and decadent texture.

Active Time 15 minutes | **Total Time** 40 minutes, plus cooling | **Makes** 16

1	15-ounce can low-sodium chickpeas, rinsed
2	tablespoons honey
2	teaspoons pure vanilla extract
1/2	cup creamy peanut butter
2/3	cup old-fashioned rolled oats
1/2	cup roasted unsalted peanuts
1	teaspoon baking powder
1/4	teaspoon baking soda
1/2	teaspoon kosher salt
1/3	cup strawberry jam

TEST KITCHEN TIP

Don't drain that can! Aquafaba, the viscous liquid surrounding the chickpeas, mimics egg whites, making it an easy vegan replacement in meringues, marshmallows or even aioli.

1. Heat oven to 350°F. Line an 8-inch square baking pan with parchment paper, leaving a 2-inch overhang on two opposite sides.

2. In a food processor, pulse chickpeas, honey and vanilla until smooth, 2 to 3 minutes. Add peanut butter and pulse to incorporate, scraping the side of the bowl as necessary.

3. In a small bowl, mix together oats, peanuts, baking powder, baking soda and salt. Add to food processor and pulse a few times until combined but chunky. Transfer 1 cup dough to a bowl and set aside.

4. Transfer remaining dough to the prepared pan and evenly press in. Gently spread jam on top, then crumble remaining dough over jam.

5. Bake until edges just pull away from the pan and the top is set and light golden brown, 25 to 30 minutes. Let cool in the pan for at least 15 minutes, then use overhangs to transfer to a cooling rack to cool completely. Cut into squares.

PER SERVING

About 140 calories, 7 g fat (1 g saturated fat), 5 g protein, 170 mg sodium, 16 g carbohydrates, 2 g fiber

Blood Orange & Olive Oil Shortbread

Pretty-in-pink bars get their gorgeous color from blood orange juice whisked with confectioners' sugar into a delicious-meets-beautiful glaze.

Active Time 15 minutes | **Total Time** 30 minutes, plus cooling | **Makes** 48

3 cups all-purpose flour

½ teaspoon kosher salt

2¼ cups confectioners' sugar

1 cup extra virgin olive oil

2 teaspoons pure vanilla extract

2 tablespoons blood orange juice

TEST
KITCHEN
TIP

Can't find blood orange juice? Sub in lime, lemon or grapefruit juice for the glaze. (Note: The color will change.)

1. Heat oven to 350°F. In a large bowl, whisk together flour, salt and 1 cup confectioners' sugar. Add oil and vanilla, and mix to combine.

2. Roll dough between 2 pieces of parchment paper to ¼ inch thick. Slide rolled dough onto a baking sheet, remove top piece of parchment and bake until edges are light golden brown, about 15 minutes. While still warm on the baking sheet, cut shortbread into 1- by 2-inch rectangles, but do not move or handle. Let cool completely, about 30 minutes.

3. In a small bowl, whisk together blood orange juice and remaining 1¼ cups confectioners' sugar. Dip cooled cookies into glaze diagonally and place on parchment to dry. Store covered at room temperature for up to a week.

PER SERVING

About 95 calories, 4.5 g fat (0.5 g saturated fat), 1 g protein, 20 mg sodium, 12 g carbohydrates, 0 g fiber

Orange-Turmeric Squares

These golden squares are all about opposites: The silky-smooth topping (made with protein-packed tofu!) contrasts the crispy crust, and the tangy orange flavor mellows the turmeric's bold taste.

Active Time 30 minutes | **Total Time** 3 hours, plus chilling | **Makes** 16

For the Crust

Nonstick cooking spray, for the pan

2 ¼ cups all-purpose flour

½ cup granulated sugar

½ teaspoon kosher salt

¾ cup olive oil

For the Filling

1 16-ounce package extra-firm silken tofu, drained

3 tablespoons orange zest

1 cup freshly squeezed orange juice (from about 4 oranges)

⅓ cup granulated sugar

½ cup cornstarch

1 teaspoon ground turmeric

1. Heat oven to 350°F. Lightly coat a 9-inch square baking pan with nonstick spray. Line with parchment paper, leaving a 2-inch overhang on two opposite sides; spray paper.

2. Make the crust: In a bowl, whisk together flour, sugar and salt. With a fork, mix in olive oil until fully incorporated. Press dough into the bottom of the prepared pan in an even layer. Using a fork, prick all over and bake until light golden brown at the edges, 40 to 45 minutes. Let cool completely. Reduce oven temperature to 300°F. While cooling, make the filling.

3. Prepare the filling: In a food processor, pulse tofu, zest, juice and sugar to combine, 4 to 5 times. In a small bowl, combine cornstarch and turmeric; sift into the food processor and pulse to combine. Pour into cooled crust and bake until edges are set, 30 to 40 minutes. Refrigerate for at least 1 hour or overnight. When ready to serve, use overhangs to transfer to a cutting board and cut into squares.

PER SERVING
About 235 calories, 11 g fat (1.5 g saturated fat), 4 g protein, 80 mg sodium, 30 g carbohydrates, 1 g fiber

INGREDIENT SPOTLIGHT

Silken Tofu

Its creamy, custard-like texture and milk flavor make it an ideal egg substitute in dense treats, like this velvety curd filling.

Brown Butter & Hazelnut Blondies

Toasty brown butter brings these blondies to a whole new level. Plus, the nutty, delectably sweet chopped hazelnuts push the flavor over the top.

Active Time 25 minutes | **Total Time** 2 hours | **Makes** 16

Nonstick cooking spray, for the pan

1½   cups all-purpose flour

1¼   teaspoons kosher salt

1   teaspoon baking powder

¾   cup (1 ½ sticks) unsalted butter

1½   cups packed dark brown sugar

1½   teaspoons pure vanilla extract

2   large eggs

1½   cups hazelnuts, toasted and coarsely chopped

1. Heat oven to 375°F. Lightly coat a 9-inch square baking pan with nonstick spray. Line with parchment paper, leaving a 2-inch overhang on two opposite sides; spray paper.

2. In a medium bowl, whisk together flour, salt and baking powder; set aside.

3. In a small saucepan, cook butter on medium-high, stirring often, until fragrant and deep golden brown, 6 to 8 minutes. Transfer browned butter to a large bowl and let cool for 10 minutes. Whisk in sugar and vanilla. Add eggs, one at a time, whisking until blended after each addition. Whisk in flour mixture. Fold in toasted hazelnuts. Transfer batter to the prepared pan.

4. Bake until a wooden pick inserted into the center comes out with a few moist crumbs attached, 24 to 26 minutes. Let cool completely in the pan. Use overhangs to transfer to a cutting board and cut into squares.

PER SERVING

About 280 calories, 16 g fat (6 g saturated fat), 4 g protein, 200 mg sodium, 31 g carbohydrates, 1 g fiber

Mom's Glazed Coffee Squares

Cookies and coffee go hand in hand...just ask anyone who dunks biscotti into their cup of joe. These bars infuse the flavor of freshly brewed coffee directly into the raisins and the glaze.

Active Time 30 minutes | **Total Time** 1 hour | **Makes** 12

For the Bars

- ½ cup brewed coffee
- ¼ cup raisins
- 2 tablespoons molasses
- ½ cup (1 stick) unsalted butter, at room temperature
- ¾ cup packed brown sugar
- 1 large egg
- 1½ cups all-purpose flour
- ¾ teaspoon ground cinnamon
- ½ teaspoon baking soda
- ½ teaspoon baking powder
- ½ teaspoon kosher salt
- ½ cup chopped walnuts

For the Glaze

- 1 cup confectioners' sugar
- 2 tablespoons brewed coffee
- ½ teaspoon pure vanilla extract
- ½ teaspoon unsalted butter, at room temperature

1. Heat oven to 350°F. Line a 9- by 13-inch baking pan with parchment paper, leaving a 2-inch overhang on the two long sides.

2. Make the bars: In a small saucepan, simmer coffee, raisins and molasses on medium until raisins plump, 10 minutes. Let cool completely.

3. Using an electric mixer, beat butter, brown sugar and egg in a large bowl on medium speed until light and fluffy, 3 minutes, scraping the bowl as needed.

4. In a medium bowl, whisk together flour, cinnamon, baking soda, baking powder and salt; add to butter mixture. Beat until just combined. Reduce speed to low and drizzle in raisin mixture; beat until blended. With spatula, fold in chopped walnuts.

5. Spread batter evenly into the prepared pan and bake until a wooden pick inserted into the center comes out clean, 13 to 15 minutes. Let cool in the pan for 10 minutes.

6. Meanwhile, make the glaze: In a bowl, stir together confectioners' sugar, coffee, vanilla and butter until smooth. Spread over warm cake and let set before cutting into squares. Store in an airtight container at room temperature for up to 3 days.

PER SERVING
About 275 calories, 12 g fat (6 g saturated fat), 3 g protein, 255 mg sodium, 42 g carbohydrates, 1 g fiber

TEST
KITCHEN
TIP

No time for the glaze
to set? Pop the bars into
the fridge for 5 minutes
to quickly harden
the icing.

White Chocolate & Peppermint Blondies

This classic flavor combination is a hit around the winter holidays, but these blondies are proof you can enjoy peppermint and chocolate at any time of the year.

Active Time 25 minutes | **Total Time** 3 hours | **Makes** 18

Nonstick cooking spray, for the pan

¾ cup (1 ½ sticks) unsalted butter, melted

¾ cup granulated sugar

⅔ cup packed light brown sugar

3 large eggs, at room temperature

¼ teaspoon pure peppermint extract

2 teaspoons pure vanilla extract

2 ⅔ cups all-purpose flour

¾ teaspoon baking powder

¼ teaspoon kosher salt

1 ½ cups coarsely chopped white chocolate

1 16-ounce package cream cheese

1 cup confectioners' sugar

¾ cup peppermints, crushed

1. Heat oven to 325°F. Lightly coat a 9- by 13-inch baking pan with nonstick cooking spray. Line pan with parchment paper, leaving a 2-inch overhang on the two long sides; spray paper.

2. In a medium bowl, whisk together butter, granulated sugar, brown sugar, eggs, peppermint extract and 1 teaspoon vanilla to combine. In another bowl, whisk together flour, baking powder and salt. Stir flour mixture into butter mixture to combine. Stir in chocolate. Spread batter in the prepared pan.

3. Bake until golden brown and a wooden pick inserted into the center comes out clean, 30 to 35 minutes. Let cool completely in the pan.

4. Using an electric mixer, beat cream cheese and confectioners' sugar in a large bowl on medium speed until light and fluffy, 1 to 2 minutes. Beat in remaining 1 teaspoon vanilla. Spread frosting on blondies; sprinkle with peppermints. Freeze until frosting is set, 30 minutes. Use overhangs to transfer to a cutting board and cut into squares.

PER SERVING

About 435 calories, 22 g fat (13 g saturated fat), 5 g protein, 155 mg sodium, 54 g carbohydrates, 1 g fiber

Toffee-Cashew Crunch Bars

This recipe for homemade toffee tastes incredible on its own, but layering it on top of a tender, buttery cookie crust makes for an irresistible, next-level dessert.

Active Time 25 minutes | **Total Time** 1 hour 15 minutes | **Makes** 36

For the Crust

½	cup (1 stick) unsalted butter, at room temperature
¼	cup granulated sugar
¼	cup packed light brown sugar
1	large egg yolk
¼	teaspoon kosher salt
1½	cups all-purpose flour

For the Filling

1	cup packed light brown sugar
½	cup (1 stick) unsalted butter
¼	cup dark or light corn syrup
½	cup heavy cream
2	teaspoons pure vanilla extract
3	cups raw cashews

1. Heat oven to 350°F. Line a 9- by 13-inch baking pan with nonstick foil, leaving a 2-inch overhang on the two long sides.

2. Make the crust: Using an electric mixer, beat butter in a large bowl on medium speed until creamy, 3 minutes. Beat in sugars, egg yolk and salt. Reduce speed to low and mix in flour (the dough will be crumbly). Press crust evenly into the bottom of the prepared pan. Bake until golden brown at edges, 25 minutes. Let cool completely in the pan.

3. Meanwhile, make the filling: In a medium saucepan, combine brown sugar, butter and corn syrup, and cook on medium, stirring occasionally, until butter melts. Bring to a full boil; boil 1½ minutes, whisking a few times. Remove the pan from heat. Stir in cream, vanilla and cashews.

4. Pour filling over cooled crust and spread evenly. Bake until filling is bubbly all over, 25 minutes. Let cool completely in the pan.

5. Use overhangs to transfer to a cutting board and cut into squares.

PER SERVING

About 170 calories, 11 g fat (5 g saturated fat), 2 g protein, 25 mg sodium, 17 g carbohydrates, 1 g fiber

Double-Stuffed Brownies

While boxed brownie mix is clutch in a chocolate craving emergency, it's easy (and so worth it) to make brownies from scratch. Up the chocolatey goodness by adding both chocolate chips *and* chocolate sandwich cookies to the batter.

Active Time 15 minutes | **Total Time** 1 hour | **Makes** 16

Nonstick cooking spray, for the pan

- 1 cup (2 sticks) unsalted butter, cut into pieces
- 1½ cups packed brown sugar
- ½ cup granulated sugar
- ½ teaspoon kosher salt
- ½ cup bittersweet chocolate chips
- 3 large eggs
- 2 teaspoons pure vanilla extract
- 1½ cups unsweetened cocoa powder
- ¾ cup all-purpose flour
- 18 chocolate sandwich cookies, roughly chopped

1. Heat oven to 350°F. Lightly coat a 9-inch square baking pan with nonstick cooking spray.

2. In a large bowl, combine butter, sugars and salt, and microwave on High in 30-second intervals, stirring between each, until butter is melted. Whisk until mixture is combined and glossy, then stir in chocolate chips, whisking to melt. Let cool, whisking occasionally, 5 minutes.

3. When butter mixture is cool, whisk in eggs, one at a time, then vanilla. Stir in cocoa and then flour until just combined. Fold in half the chopped sandwich cookies, then transfer batter to the prepared pan. Scatter remaining cookies on top.

4. Bake until set and a wooden pick inserted 2 inches from the center comes out with a few moist crumbs attached, 35 to 45 minutes. Cut into squares.

PER SERVING
About 360 calories, 19 g fat (10.5 g saturated fat), 4 g protein, 135 mg sodium, 48 g carbohydrates, 4 g fiber

Fudgy Beet Brownies

These lightened-up brownies received rave reviews. The secret? Veggies in baked goods help cut added sugar by half — without sacrificing texture or flavor.

Active Time 20 minutes | **Total Time** 50 minutes | **Makes** 16

Nonstick cooking spray, for the pan

½   cup (1 stick) unsalted butter

6   ounces bittersweet chocolate, chopped

½   cup firmly packed brown sugar

8   ounces cooked, peeled whole beets (about 4 small), pureed in blender or food processor

1   teaspoon pure vanilla extract

1   teaspoon espresso powder

¼   teaspoon kosher salt

2   large eggs, at room temperature

½   cup white whole-wheat flour

1. Heat oven to 350°F. Lightly coat an 8-inch square baking pan with nonstick spray. Line with parchment paper, leaving a 2-inch overhang on two opposite sides; spray paper.

2. In a medium saucepan, melt butter and chocolate on low, stirring occasionally, until smooth. Remove from heat, cool slightly, then whisk in sugar, beets, vanilla, espresso powder and salt. Whisk in eggs, one at a time, until fully incorporated. Fold in flour until just combined.

3. Pour batter into the prepared pan and bake until a knife inserted into the center comes out clean or with just a few moist crumbs attached, 30 to 35 minutes. Let cool in the pan for 10 minutes, then use overhangs to transfer to a cutting board and cut into squares.

PER SERVING

About 160 calories, 11 g fat (6.5 g saturated fat), 3 g protein, 55 mg sodium, 16 g carbohydrates, 2 g fiber

= INGREDIENT =
SPOTLIGHT

Beets

Handling beets can be a messy job. To avoid stains, cover your work surface with waxed paper before you begin prepping and wear disposable gloves.

Avocado Brownies

Another healthier take on brownies, this version subs in fresh avocado for butter or oil. Since the fruit is high in unsaturated fat and has a creamy texture, you won't miss the butter one bit. (See photo, page 112.)

Active Time 15 minutes | **Total Time** 50 minutes | **Makes** 16

Nonstick cooking spray, for the pan

4 ounces dark chocolate, chopped

½ cup almond flour

½ cup all-purpose flour

¼ cup unsweetened cocoa powder

½ teaspoon baking powder

½ teaspoon kosher salt

3 large eggs

1 cup granulated sugar

1 teaspoon pure vanilla extract

½ cup mashed avocado (from 1 avocado)

1. Heat oven to 350°F. Lightly coat an 8-inch square baking pan with nonstick spray. Line with parchment paper, leaving a 2-inch overhang on two opposite sides; spray paper.

2. In a small bowl, microwave chocolate on 50 percent power in 30-second intervals, stirring between each, until melted and smooth, 1 to 2 minutes.

3 In a food processor, pulse flours, cocoa powder, baking powder and salt to combine, 4 or 5 times. Add eggs, sugar and vanilla, and pulse to incorporate. Add avocado, then melted chocolate, and process until just blended.

4. Transfer batter to the prepared pan and bake until a wooden a pick inserted into the center comes out with moist crumbs attached, 20 to 25 minutes.

5. Let cool for at least 10 minutes, then use overhangs to transfer to a cutting board and cut into squares.

PER SERVING

About 155 calories, 7 g fat (2.5 g saturated fat), 3 g protein, 105 mg sodium, 21 g carbohydrates, 2 g fiber

Cookie Cheat!

Start with a box of **brownie mix** and replace the butter or oil with an equal amount of **pureed avocado**.

Lemon & Poppy Seed Bars

For an easy upgrade to your standard lemon bars, fold poppy seeds into the crust.

Active Time 15 minutes | **Total Time** 1 hour 10 minutes | **Makes** 48

- 1 tablespoon poppy seeds
- ¼ teaspoon kosher salt
- 3 cups all-purpose flour
- 2 tablespoons grated lemon zest
- 1 cup (2 sticks) unsalted butter, at room temperature
- 3 cups granulated sugar
- 8 large eggs
- 1 cup freshly squeezed lemon juice

  Confectioners' sugar, for dusting

1. Heat oven to 350°F. Line a 9- by 13-inch baking pan with parchment paper, leaving a 2-inch overhang on the two long sides.

2. In a large bowl, whisk together the poppy seeds, salt, 2 cups flour and 1 tablespoon zest; set aside.

3. Using an electric mixer, beat butter and ½ cup granulated sugar in a second large bowl on medium speed until light and fluffy, 3 minutes. Reduce speed to low and gradually add flour mixture, mixing until just incorporated. Press mixture into the prepared pan. Bake until light golden brown, 15 to 20 minutes.

4. In a third large bowl, whisk together eggs, lemon juice and remaining 2½ cups granulated sugar, 1 cup flour and 1 tablespoon zest. Spread over hot crust and bake until set, 30 to 35 minutes. Let cool completely in the pan.

5. Use overhangs to transfer to a cutting board. Cut into 1½-inch squares and dust with confectioners' sugar.

PER SERVING
About 130 calories, 5 g fat (3 g saturated fat), 2 g protein, 25 mg sodium, 20 g carbohydrates, 0 g fiber

TEST KITCHEN TIP

When zesting lemons, it is important to remove *just* the flavorful colored part of the citrus skin, avoiding the bitter white pith underneath.

Cherry Linzer Bars

Love traditional linzer cookies? You can get that jam-packed, sugar-dusted cookie flavor without chilling or rolling out any dough. Enter this easy, pat-in-the-pan linzer bar.

Active Time 45 minutes | **Total Time** 1 hour 20 minutes, plus cooling | **Makes** 36

½ cup dried tart cherries

2 tablespoons water

1 ¾ cups all-purpose flour

1 teaspoon ground cinnamon

½ teaspoon baking powder

¼ teaspoon kosher salt

1 cup hazelnuts, toasted, skins rubbed off

½ cup granulated sugar

½ cup packed light brown sugar

¾ cup (1 ½ sticks) unsalted butter, softened

½ teaspoon freshly grated lemon peel

1 large egg

1 12-ounce jar tart cherry jam

Confectioners' sugar, for garnish

1. Heat oven to 350°F. In a small bowl, combine cherries and water; microwave on High, 1 minute. Set aside.

2. Meanwhile, line a 9- by 13-inch baking pan with parchment paper, leaving a 2-inch overhang on the two long sides. On waxed paper, combine flour, cinnamon, baking powder and salt.

3. In a food processor, pulse hazelnuts and sugars until nuts are finely ground, 8 to 12 times. Add butter and lemon peel; pulse until creamy. Blend in egg. Add flour mixture; pulse just until mixture comes together.

4. Transfer 1¼ cups dough to a bowl and refrigerate until ready to use. With floured fingers, press remaining dough into the bottom of the prepared pan. Stir jam into cherries, then spread over crust, up to ¼ inch from edges.

5. Using your hands, roll chilled dough into ¼-inch-thick ropes and arrange them diagonally, 1½ inches apart, over jam. Arrange remaining ropes around the edge of the pan. Bake until dough is golden brown, 35 minutes. Let cool completely in the pan.

6. Use overhangs to transfer to a cutting board and cut into squares. Store in airtight containers, layered with parchment paper, at room temperature for up to 3 days or in the freezer for up to a month. Sprinkle with confectioners' sugar before serving.

PER SERVING
About 135 calories, 6 g fat (3 g saturated fat), 2 g protein, 25 mg sodium, 19 g carbohydrates, 1 g fiber

Cranberry Swirl Cheesecake Bars

All the creamy deliciousness of cheesecake, none of the tricky baking techniques (read: no water bath). Another delightful change: Chocolate wafer cookies make this crust instead of graham crackers.

Active Time 30 minutes | **Total Time** 1 hour 40 minutes | **Makes** 12

½ cup cranberries (thawed if frozen)

½ cup frozen raspberries, thawed

1 teaspoon freshly grated orange zest, plus ¼ cup orange juice

1 cup granulated sugar

4 tablespoons (½ stick) unsalted butter, melted, plus more for the pan

1 9-ounce package chocolate wafer cookies

3 8-ounce packages cream cheese, at room temperature

¾ cup sour cream

2 tablespoons all-purpose flour

2 teaspoons pure vanilla extract

3 large eggs

1. In a medium saucepan, combine cranberries, raspberries, orange zest, juice and ¼ cup sugar. Simmer, stirring occasionally, until cranberries burst and sauce thickens, 5 to 7 minutes. Transfer mixture to a food processor and puree until smooth. Strain into a medium bowl; let cool for 10 minutes, then refrigerate until ready to use.

2. Heat oven to 375°F. Grease a 9- by 13-inch baking pan. In a clean food processor, pulse chocolate wafers into fine crumbs. Add melted butter and pulse to incorporate. Press crumb mixture into the bottom and 2½ inches up the sides of the pan. Bake until crust is set and fragrant, 10 to 12 minutes. Transfer to a cooling rack to cool. Reduce oven temperature to 325°F.

3. While crust is cooling, using an electric mixer, beat together cream cheese, sour cream, flour, vanilla and remaining ¾ cup sugar in a large bowl until smooth. Beat in eggs, one at a time. Transfer ½ cup filling to a bowl; set aside. Pour remaining filling into cooled crust.

4. Whisk reserved filling into cranberry mixture (it will be thin), then transfer to a resealable plastic bag. Snip a tiny corner off the bag and pipe lines lengthwise over batter. Drag a skewer across lines to form a pattern. Bake until cheesecake is just set (center should still wobble slightly), 18 to 20 minutes. Let cool completely, then refrigerate for at least 3 hours before cutting into bars.

PER SERVING
About 450 calories, 30 g fat (17 g saturated fat), 7 g protein, 355 mg sodium, 39 g carbohydrates, 1 g fiber

Chapter 5

Spectacular Cookie Creations

Sometimes two cookies are better than one — especially when there's a decadent caramel sauce, chocolate frosting or scoops of ice cream between them! This chapter showcases everything from whoopie pies to melty s'mores, plus lots of other delicious ways to get baking.

CHOCOLATE CHIP TRIPLE-DECKER CAKE 176

←

Alfajores

A coffee-shop staple in Argentina, these treats are a caramel-filled delight. Layer your cookie sandwiches with store-bought dulce de leche or make a batch in your slow cooker. For a more traditional take, roll the edges of the caramel filling in shredded sweetened coconut.

Active Time 40 minutes | **Total Time** 1 hour, plus cooling | **Makes** 36

1   cup all-purpose flour,
    plus more for surfaces

1 2/3   cups cornstarch

1   teaspoon baking powder

3/4   teaspoon ground cinnamon

1/4   teaspoon kosher salt

10   tablespoons unsalted butter,
    at room temperature

1/2   cup sugar

1/2   teaspoon pure vanilla extract

4   large egg yolks

1   16-ounce jar store-bought
    dulce de leche or about
    1 cup Slow-Cooker Dulce de Leche

Bonus Recipe!

Slow-Cooker Dulce de Leche

Transfer **1 can (14 ounces) sweetened condensed milk** to one 1-cup canning jar or three 1/3-cup jars. Stir in **1/8 teaspoon salt** and seal tightly with lid; place in the bowl of a slow cooker (if using a larger jar, lay it down sideways). Cover with water. Place the lid on the slow cooker and cook on Low for 8 hours. Carefully remove the jar from water and wipe dry. Let cool for 1 hour in the refrigerator before opening. Makes about 1 cup.

1. Heat oven to 350°F. Line 2 baking sheets with parchment paper.

2. Into a large bowl, sift flour, cornstarch, baking powder, cinnamon and salt; set aside.

3. Using an electric mixer, beat butter and sugar in a large bowl on medium-high speed until creamy, about 3 minutes. Beat in vanilla, then egg yolks, one at a time. Reduce speed to low, then add flour mixture until just combined.

4. On a lightly floured surface, with a lightly floured rolling pin, roll half the dough to 1/4 inch thick. With a 1 1/2-inch round cutter, cut out rounds. With a small knife or mini offset spatula, place cookies onto the prepared sheets, spacing them 1 inch apart. Reroll scraps once and cut out more rounds.

5. Bake until golden brown on bottom, 12 to 15 minutes. Let cool on baking sheets for 5 minutes before transferring to a cooling rack to cool completely. Repeat with remaining rounds.

6. Assemble sandwiches: Place dulce de leche in a piping bag fitted with a star tip, pipe onto half the cookies, then top with remaining cookies. Cookie sandwiches can be stored in airtight containers in the freezer for up to a month.

PER SERVING

About 120 calories, 5 g fat (3 g saturated fat), 2 g protein, 75 mg sodium, 18 g carbohydrates, 0 g fiber

Switch It Up!
Not a fan of caramel?
Sub in hazelnut-cocoa spread for
the dulce de leche.

Ginger & Cream Sandwich Bites

Though tiny, these cookie sandwiches are brimming with flavor — thanks to fresh grated ginger in the chewy bite-sized cookies and orange zest in the buttercream filling.

Active Time 30 minutes | **Total Time** 2 hours, plus chilling and cooling | **Makes** 80

For the Cookies

2 ¾ cups all-purpose flour

1 teaspoon baking powder

1 teaspoon baking soda

¼ teaspoon kosher salt

¾ cup (1 ½ sticks) unsalted butter, at room temperature

1 ½ cups sugar

1 large egg

¼ cup molasses

1 tablespoon grated peeled fresh ginger

For the Filling

½ cup (1 stick) unsalted butter, at room temperature

1 teaspoon orange zest

2 cups confectioners' sugar, sifted

1 tablespoon heavy cream

≈ INGREDIENT ≈
SPOTLIGHT

Molasses

During the sugar-refining process, the juice that is extracted from sugarcane is boiled down to a syrupy mixture from which sugar crystals are removed. The remaining syrup is molasses.

1. Prepare the cookies: In a medium bowl, whisk together flour, baking powder, baking soda and salt; set aside.

2. Using an electric mixer, beat butter and 1 cup sugar in a large bowl on medium speed until light and fluffy, about 3 minutes. Beat in egg, molasses and ginger. Reduce speed to low and gradually add flour mixture, mixing until just incorporated (dough will be soft). Cover and refrigerate until firm enough to handle, about 1 hour.

3. Heat oven to 350°F. Line 2 large baking sheets with parchment paper. Place remaining ½ cup sugar in a small bowl. Working with one baking sheet at a time and keeping dough covered, roll ½ teaspoon dough into a ball and then roll in sugar to coat. Place balls onto the prepared sheet, spacing them 1 inch apart. Freeze until firm, about 15 minutes. Repeat with remaining dough.

4. Bake until cookies are puffed and set, 8 to 10 minutes, rotating the positions of the baking sheets halfway through. Let cool on baking sheets for 2 minutes, then slide parchment paper with cookies onto a cooling rack to cool completely.

5. Meanwhile, make the filling: Using an electric mixer, beat butter in a large bowl on medium speed until creamy, 2 minutes. Add orange zest. Reduce speed to low and gradually add confectioners' sugar, then beat in heavy cream.

6. Once cookies are cool, assemble sandwiches: Spread a small amount of filling onto half the cookies, then top with remaining cookies.

PER SERVING

About 70 calories, 3 g fat (2 g saturated fat), 1 g protein, 30 mg sodium, 11 g carbohydrates, 0 g fiber

GIFT IT!
Line a clear food-safe box with patterned paper, add cookies and close. Tie with a ribbon for an extra pop of color.

Oatmeal Cream Pies

Psst! These lightened-up cookies are made with less butter than traditional recipes and an airy seven-minute frosting whipped with egg whites.

Active Time 40 minutes | **Total Time** 1 hour | **Makes** 10

For the Cookies

1 ½	cups quick-cooking oats
1 ½	cups all-purpose flour
1	teaspoon baking soda
1	teaspoon cinnamon
½	teaspoon kosher salt
½	cup firmly packed dark brown sugar
½	cup granulated sugar
½	cup (1 stick) unsalted butter, melted
1	large egg yolk
1	teaspoon pure vanilla extract
½	cup water

For the Filling

1	large egg white
3	tablespoons granulated sugar
⅛	teaspoon cream of tartar
¼	teaspoon pure vanilla extract

TEST KITCHEN TIP

You need only 1 large egg total for this recipe: Separate the egg and use the yolk for the cookies and the white for the filling. Eggs separate most easily when cold.

1. Heat oven to 375°F. Line 2 baking sheets with parchment paper. In a large bowl, whisk together oats, flour, baking soda, cinnamon and salt; set aside.

2. In a second bowl, whisk together sugars, butter, egg yolk, vanilla and water. Add flour mixture and mix until combined.

3. Drop cookies (2 tablespoons each) onto the prepared sheets, spacing them 2 inches apart. Use your hands to flatten to ½-inch thickness and 2-inch diameter. Bake until edges are golden brown, 9 to 12 minutes, rotating the positions of the baking sheets halfway through. Let cool on baking sheets on a cooling rack for 5 minutes. Slide parchment with cookies onto cooling rack to cool completely.

4. Meanwhile, make the filling: In a large bowl, whisk together egg white, sugar and cream of tartar. Set the bowl over a saucepan of simmering water (not touching water) and cook, whisking constantly, until sugar is dissolved and egg white is very warm to the touch, about 2 minutes.

5. Using an electric mixer, whisk warm egg-white mixture on medium speed until glossy and soft peaks form, 2 to 3 minutes. Add vanilla.

6. Once cookies are cool, assemble sandwiches: Spread filling onto bottom of half the cookies, then top with remaining cookies.

PER SERVING

About 300 calories, 11 g fat (6 g saturated fat), 4 g protein, 235 mg sodium, 48 g carbohydrates, 2 g fiber

Jammy Sandwiches

Taking a cue from traditional Austrian linzer cookies, these treats have cutouts in the top layer to showcase the bright, tangy jam filling and are finished with plenty of powdered sugar.

Active Time 40 minutes | **Total Time** 1 hour, plus chilling and cooling | **Makes** 48

2 ¾ cups all-purpose flour

1 teaspoon ground cinnamon

½ teaspoon ground nutmeg

½ teaspoon baking powder

¼ teaspoon ground cloves

¼ teaspoon kosher salt

1 cup (2 sticks) unsalted butter, at room temperature

¾ cup granulated sugar

1 large egg plus 1 egg yolk

2 teaspoons pure vanilla extract

2 teaspoons finely grated orange zest

1 ½ cups apricot or raspberry jam

Confectioners' sugar, for dusting

Bonus Recipe!

10-Minute Berry Jam

In a large bowl, mash **2 cups berries** and **⅓ cup sugar**. Microwave, uncovered, on High for 10 minutes, stirring once. Let cool completely. Makes ¾ cup.

1. In a large bowl, whisk together flour, cinnamon, nutmeg, baking powder, cloves and salt; set aside.

2. Using an electric mixer, beat butter and sugar in another large bowl on medium speed until light and fluffy, about 3 minutes. Beat in egg and yolk, then vanilla and zest.

3. Reduce speed to low and gradually add flour mixture, mixing until just incorporated. Shape dough into 4 disks and roll each between 2 sheets of parchment paper to ⅛-inch thickness. Chill until firm, 30 minutes in the refrigerator or 15 minutes in the freezer.

4. Heat oven to 350°F. Line 2 baking sheets with parchment paper. Using floured 2- to 3-inch round fluted cutters, cut out cookies. Place cookies onto the prepared baking sheets, spacing them 2 inches apart. Using a smaller cutter, cut out centers from half the cookies. Reroll, chill and cut scraps.

5. Bake until cookies are light golden brown around edges, 10 to 12 minutes, rotating the positions of the baking sheets halfway through. Let cool on baking sheets for 5 minutes before transferring to a cooling rack to cool completely.

6. Once cookies are cool, spread 1½ teaspoons jam onto each whole cookie. Dust cutout cookies with confectioners' sugar, then place on top of jam-covered cookies.

PER SERVING

About 100 calories, 4 g fat (2.5 g saturated fat), 1 g protein, 20 mg sodium, 16 g carbohydrates, 0 g fiber

GIFT IT!
Use sturdy cardstock paper for makeshift boxes: Cut paper into the shape of a four-point star, fold in the corners and seal with a sticker. Tip: Add a layer of waxed paper to protect the cookie.

Apple Pie Rugelach

Traditionally made with a cream cheese dough, this Jewish pastry provides nearly endless possibilities for flavor and filling combinations. Here, dried apples, apple jelly, cinnamon and walnuts are rolled into the dough for a treat that is warm, inviting and reminiscent of fall.

Active Time 1 hour 30 minutes | **Total Time** 2 hours, plus chilling and cooling | **Makes** 64

For the Dough

- 1 cup (2 sticks) unsalted butter, at room temperature
- 1 8-ounce package cream cheese, at room temperature
- 2 cups all-purpose flour
- ½ teaspoon kosher salt

For the Filling

- 4 ounces dried apples, finely chopped (1½ cups)
- ½ cup walnuts, finely chopped
- ¼ cup packed brown sugar
- 1 cup granulated sugar
- 2 teaspoons ground cinnamon
- ¾ cup apple jelly
- Confectioners' sugar, for dusting

1. Make the dough: Using an electric mixer, beat butter and cream cheese in a large bowl on medium speed until creamy, about 3 minutes. Reduce speed to low and beat in flour and salt until just incorporated. Divide dough into 4 equal portions; flatten each into a disk. Wrap each disk in plastic wrap and refrigerate for at least 4 hours or overnight.

2. Heat oven to 350°F. Line 2 large baking sheets with parchment paper.

3. Prepare the filling: In a medium bowl, combine apples, walnuts and brown sugar; set aside.

4. In a small bowl, combine sugar and cinnamon. Sprinkle a work surface with 2 tablespoons cinnamon sugar. Place a disk of dough on top of cinnamon sugar, then turn over to coat both sides. Roll dough into a 10-inch round, turning over a few times and sprinkling with 2 more tablespoons cinnamon sugar to coat both sides.

5. Spread top of round with 3 tablespoons jelly, then sprinkle with ½ cup filling, leaving a ½-inch border around edge. Using a knife, cut dough into 16 equal wedges. Starting at wide end, roll up each wedge jelly-roll fashion. Place rugelach onto prepared sheets, point side down, spacing them 1 inch apart.

6. Bake until browned and cooked through, 30 to 33 minutes. Immediately transfer to a cooling rack to cool completely. Repeat with remaining dough, cinnamon sugar, jelly and filling. Store cookies in airtight containers at room temperature for up to a week or in the freezer for up to 3 months. Dust with confectioners' sugar before serving.

PER SERVING
About 90 calories, 5 g fat (3 g saturated fat), 1 g protein, 40 mg sodium, 11 g carbohydrates, 0 g fiber

GLUTEN FREE RECIPE

PB & Grape Jamwiches

For a sweet twist on the lunchbox favorite, layer grape jam between two mini chewy PB cookies.

Active Time 40 minutes | **Total Time** 1 hour 15 minutes, including cooling | **Makes** 30

1	cup creamy peanut butter
¾	cup packed light brown sugar
1	large egg
¾	teaspoon baking soda
½	cup peanuts, finely chopped
½	cup Concord grape jam

1. Heat oven to 350°F. Line 2 or 3 large baking sheets with parchment paper. Using an electric mixer, beat peanut butter, brown sugar, egg and baking soda in a large bowl on medium speed until fully incorporated, about 2 minutes.

2. Roll dough into ¾-inch balls (about a level teaspoon each) and coat half the balls with chopped nuts. Place balls onto the prepared sheets, spacing them 2 inches apart.

3. Bake until cookies are puffed and starting to turn light golden brown around edges, 8 to 10 minutes. Let cool on baking sheets for 5 minutes before transferring to a cooling rack to cool completely. Repeat with any remaining balls, if necessary.

4. Assemble sandwiches: Spread ½ teaspoon jam onto bottom of each plain cookie, then top with a nut-coated cookie.

PER SERVING
About 90 calories, 5 g fat (1 g saturated fat), 2 g protein, 70 mg sodium, 11 g carbohydrates, 1 g fiber

Mini Chocolate Chip Sandwiches

This dessert is a cross between cake and cookies, so you get the best of both worlds: Cakier cookies are held together with a decadent chocolate frosting.

Active Time 25 minutes | **Total Time** 35 minutes | **Makes** 25

1 ½   cups cake flour

½   teaspoon baking powder

½   teaspoon baking soda

½   teaspoon kosher salt

½   cup (1 stick) unsalted butter, at room temperature

¼   cup plus 2 tablespoons granulated sugar

2   tablespoons packed brown sugar

1   large egg

½   teaspoon pure vanilla extract

4   ounces bittersweet chocolate, roughly chopped

4   ounces semisweet chocolate, roughly chopped

Chocolate frosting, for assembly

1. Line 2 large baking sheets with parchment paper. In a medium bowl, sift together cake flour, baking powder, baking soda and salt; set aside.

2. Using an electric mixer, beat butter and sugars in a large bowl on medium speed until light and fluffy, 3 minutes. Reduce speed to low and beat in egg, followed by vanilla. Add flour mixture in 3 additions, mixing until just incorporated. Fold in chocolates.

3. Scoop rounded teaspoonfuls of dough onto the prepared baking sheets, spacing them 2 inches apart. Flatten tops slightly with your hands and freeze for 10 minutes.

4. Heat oven to 350°F. Bake, rotating the positions of the baking sheets after 5 minutes, until cookies are puffed and edges are beginning to turn golden brown, 7 to 8 minutes total. Let cookies cool completely on a cooling rack.

5. Assemble sandwiches: Spread chocolate frosting onto bottom of half the cookies, then top with remaining cookies.

PER SERVING

About 155 calories, 8.5 g fat (5 g saturated fat), 2 g protein, 90 mg sodium, 19 g carbohydrates, 1 g fiber

Bonus Recipe!

Chocolate Frosting

Using an electric mixer, beat **¾ cup unsalted butter** (at room temperature), **2 cups confectioners' sugar**, **1 teaspoon pure vanilla extract** and **pinch kosher salt** in a large bowl on low speed until almost combined, about 2 to 3 minutes. Add **4 ounces semisweet chocolate** (melted and cooled) and **2 ounces unsweetened chocolate** (melted and cooled). Increase speed to high, then beat frosting until light and fluffy, 1 minute. Makes 2½ cups.

German Chocolate Sandwich Cookies

Despite its name, German Chocolate Cake is an American creation that became popular in Texas in the 1950s after a recipe for the dessert was published in a Dallas newspaper. These cookies — featuring sweetened chocolate, toasted pecans and coconut — take inspiration from that beloved cake recipe.

Active Time 50 minutes | **Total Time** 50 minutes, plus cooling | **Makes** 16

For the Filling

- 1 14-ounce can sweetened condensed milk
- 3 large egg yolks
- ½ cup (1 stick) unsalted butter, cut into pieces
- 1 teaspoon pure vanilla extract
- 1 cup chopped toasted pecans
- 1 cup shredded sweetened coconut

For the Cookies

- 2 ½ cups all-purpose flour
- ⅓ cup unsweetened cocoa powder
- 1 teaspoon baking soda
- ½ teaspoon kosher salt
- 1 cup (2 sticks) unsalted butter, melted
- 1 ½ cups packed light brown sugar
- 2 large eggs
- 2 teaspoons pure vanilla extract
- 1 ¾ cups shredded sweetened coconut (¾ cup untoasted and 1 cup toasted)
- ¾ cup chopped toasted pecans
- 4 ounces German chocolate, chopped

1. Prepare the filling: In a medium saucepan, whisk together condensed milk, egg yolks and butter, and cook on medium, whisking constantly, until bubbly and thick, 4 to 6 minutes. Remove from heat and stir in vanilla, pecans and coconut. Transfer to a bowl and let stand until cool, about 1 hour.

2. Make the cookies: Heat oven to 375°F. Line 2 baking sheets with parchment paper. In a medium bowl, whisk together flour, cocoa powder, baking soda and salt; set aside.

3. Using an electric mixer, beat butter and brown sugar in a large bowl on medium speed until combined, about 1 minute. Beat in eggs and vanilla. Reduce speed to low and beat in flour mixture until just combined. Stir in untoasted coconut, pecans and chopped chocolate.

4. Scoop mounds of dough (about 2 tablespoons each) onto the prepared sheets, spacing them 2 inches apart. Press to flatten slightly. Bake until edges are set, 8 to 10 minutes. Let cool on baking sheets for 5 minutes before transferring to a cooling rack to cool completely.

5. Assemble sandwiches: Spoon filling onto bottom of half the cookies, then top with remaining cookies. Roll edges in toasted coconut before serving.

PER SERVING

About 610 calories, 38 g fat (20 g saturated fat), 8 g protein, 230 mg sodium, 64 g carbohydrates, 4 g fiber

TEST
KITCHEN
TIP

Toast coconut the easy way:
Spread shredded coconut on a
plate, then microwave on High
for 30 seconds. Stir, then cook
2 minutes, stirring every
30 seconds, until
golden brown.

Pecan Lace Cookie Sandwiches

Crunchy, sweet and buttery, these cookies would be divine on their own — but paired up with a creamy, citrus-flecked filling, they're an absolute dream.

Active Time 30 minutes | **Total Time** 1 hour | **Makes** 24

For the Cookies

- ½ cup firmly packed dark brown sugar
- 2 tablespoons heavy cream
- 3 tablespoons unsalted butter, at room temperature
- ¼ cup all-purpose flour
- ¼ teaspoon kosher salt
- 1 cup pecans, finely chopped

For the Filling

- 1 8-ounce package cream cheese, at room temperature
- 6 tablespoons confectioners' sugar
- 2 teaspoons orange zest
- 4 tablespoons (½ stick) unsalted butter, at room temperature

1. Heat oven to 350°F. Line 2 baking sheets with parchment paper. In a medium saucepan, combine brown sugar, cream and butter. Cook on medium-low, stirring occasionally, until butter has melted, sugar has dissolved and mixture is smooth, 3 to 4 minutes. Remove from heat and stir in flour and salt, and then pecans.

2. Drop level teaspoonfuls of dough onto the prepared sheets, spacing them 3 inches apart. Bake until golden brown, 8 to 9 minutes. Let cool on baking sheets until set, 8 minutes, before transferring to a cooling rack to cool completely.

3. Meanwhile, make the filling: Using an electric mixer, beat cream cheese, confectioners' sugar, orange zest and butter in a medium bowl on medium speed until light and fluffy, about 3 minutes.

4. Assemble sandwiches: Gently spread a slightly rounded teaspoonful of filling onto bottom of half the cookies, then top with remaining cookies. Serve immediately.

PER SERVING

About 125 calories, 10 g fat (5 g saturated fat), 1 g protein, 55 mg sodium, 8 g carbohydrates, 0 g fiber

TEST KITCHEN TIP

To make ahead, store the cookies and filling separately, then assemble just before serving. The cookies can be stored in airtight containers at room temperature for up to a week. The filling can be kept in the fridge for up to 3 days.

Chocolate-Caramel S'mores

The ultimate campfire treat starts with homemade honey graham crackers. Add a drizzle of caramel sauce before sandwiching with toasted marshmallows and chocolate squares.

Active Time 30 minutes | **Total Time** 1 hour, plus chilling and cooling | **Makes** 18

1 ½   cups all-purpose flour, plus more for the surface

1   cup whole-wheat flour

½   teaspoon baking soda

½   teaspoon kosher salt

¼   teaspoon ground cinnamon

¼   cup whole milk

2   teaspoons pure vanilla extract

½   cup (1 stick) unsalted butter, at room temperature

¾   cup packed light brown sugar

3   tablespoons honey

Toasted marshmallows, for serving

Chocolate squares, for serving

Caramel sauce, for serving

1. Line 2 large baking sheets with parchment paper. In a large bowl, whisk flours, baking soda, salt and cinnamon; set aside. In a cup, combine milk and vanilla.

2. Using an electric mixer, beat butter, brown sugar and honey in another large bowl on medium-high speed until light and fluffy, about 3 minutes. Reduce speed to medium-low. Alternately add flour mixture and milk mixture, beginning and ending with flour. Increase speed to medium; beat 1 minute or until mixture forms a smooth, shiny dough.

3. Transfer half the dough to a large piece of flour-dusted parchment paper; pat and shape into a flat disk. Lightly dust disk with flour and cover with another large piece of parchment paper; with a rolling pin, roll out the dough until ⅛ inch thick. Transfer dough to a large baking sheet. Repeat with remaining dough. Refrigerate until firm, 1 hour.

4. With a 2½-inch fluted square cookie cutter, cut dough into squares (or use a fluted pastry wheel). Transfer cookies to the prepared sheets. With a fork, prick each cracker. Refrigerate until firm, 30 minutes.

5. Heat oven to 350°F. Bake crackers until golden brown, 15 to 20 minutes, rotating the positions of the baking sheets halfway through. Let cool on baking sheets for 3 minutes before transferring to a cooling rack to cool completely. Store graham crackers in an airtight container for up to 5 days or freeze for up to a month.

6. Assemble s'mores: Sandwich 1 toasted marshmallow, 1 chocolate square and 1 spoonful caramel sauce between 2 graham crackers.

PER SERVING

About 275 calories, 11 g fat (7 g saturated fat), 3 g protein, 125 mg sodium, 43 g carbohydrates, 1 g fiber

Cookie Cheat!

Upgrade your s'mores by swapping out graham crackers for your favorite store-bought cookies: Chewy chocolate chip cookies work well with toasted marshmallows and sliced strawberries, while chocolate wafer cookies pair beautifully with cinnamon-dusted toasted marshmallows and squares of melty milk chocolate.

Cinnamon-Sugar Sandwiches with Fluffy Maple Filling

Think outside the bowl with this deliciously inventive twist on a beloved breakfast food. Sugary cinnamon cereal is blended into cookie dough and also pressed onto the edges of the cookie sandwiches, so you can milk every last bite.

Active Time 1 hour | **Total Time** 3 hours | **Makes** 24

For the Cookies

2 ½ cups cinnamon crunch cereal, plus more lightly crushed for rolling

2 ¼ cups all-purpose flour

1 teaspoon baking soda

½ teaspoon kosher salt

2 teaspoons cream of tartar

1 cup (2 sticks) unsalted butter, at room temperature

1 ¾ cups sugar

2 large eggs

2 tablespoons ground cinnamon

For the Filling

½ cup (1 stick) unsalted butter, at room temperature

2 cups confectioners' sugar

3 tablespoons maple syrup

½ teaspoon ground cinnamon

½ teaspoon kosher salt

1 7-ounce jar marshmallow cream

1. In a food processor, pulse cereal until fine crumbs form, about 8 to 10 times (you should have 1¼ cups). In a medium bowl, whisk together flour, baking soda, salt and cream of tartar; set aside.

2. Using an electric mixer, beat butter and 1½ cups sugar in a large bowl on medium speed until light and fluffy, 3 to 4 minutes. Add eggs, one at a time, beating until just blended after each addition. Reduce speed to low and gradually add flour mixture. Add ¾ cup finely crushed cereal, mixing until just combined. Cover and refrigerate dough for 2 hours or up to 3 days.

3. Heat oven to 350°F. Line 2 baking sheets with parchment paper. In a small bowl, stir together cinnamon, remaining ½ cup crushed cereal and remaining ¼ cup sugar. Measure level tablespoonfuls of dough; roll into balls. Drop dough balls into the cereal-sugar mixture and roll to coat. Place balls onto the prepared sheets, spacing them 3 inches apart.

4. Bake, in batches, until golden brown on edges but still slightly soft in the center, 10 to 11 minutes. Transfer cookies to a cooling rack to cool completely.

5. Meanwhile, make the filling: Using an electric mixer, beat butter in a large bowl on medium speed until creamy, 1 to 2 minutes. Slowly add confectioners' sugar, maple syrup, cinnamon and salt, mixing until smooth, 1 to 2 minutes. Fold in marshmallow cream until just combined.

6. Assemble sandwiches: Spread filling onto bottom of half the cookies, dividing evenly, then top with remaining cookies. Roll edges of cookies in crushed cereal.

PER SERVING
About 300 calories, 13 g fat (7 g saturated fat), 2 g protein, 175 mg sodium, 46 g carbohydrates, 1 g fiber

Biscuit & Jam Cookies

You can't beat fresh-from-the-oven biscuits with homemade jam at brunch. This recipe is a riff on that classic pairing, featuring buttery, biscuit-like cookies and a sweet strawberry jam filling.

Active Time 30 minutes | **Total Time** 1 hour 30 minutes | **Makes** 20

3 ½   cups plus 2 tablespoons cake flour, plus more for the surface

½   cup granulated sugar

½   cup packed light brown sugar

2   tablespoons baking powder

1   teaspoon baking soda

1   teaspoon kosher salt

1   cup (2 sticks) cold unsalted butter, cut up

1   cup large unsweetened coconut flakes

1   large egg

½   cup heavy cream

2   teaspoons raw sugar

½   cup strawberry jam

1. Heat oven to 425°F, placing racks in the upper and lower thirds of the oven. Line 2 baking sheets with parchment paper.

2. In a food processor, place cake flour, sugars, baking powder, baking soda and salt; pulse to combine, 4 to 6 times. Add butter and coconut, and pulse just until mixture resembles coarse meal, 15 to 25 times. In a medium bowl, whisk together egg and cream; reserve 2 tablespoons. Add remaining egg mixture to butter mixture and pulse just until mixture begins to pull away from the side of the bowl, 20 to 30 times.

3. Turn dough out onto a lightly floured surface and knead gently to bring dough together, 4 to 6 times. Pat dough to ¼ inch thick and cut out cookies with a 2½-inch cookie cutter. Brush one side of cookies with reserved egg mixture and sprinkle with raw sugar. Place cookies onto the prepared sheets, spacing them 1 inch apart.

4. Bake, rotating the positions of the baking sheets halfway through, until golden brown, 7 to 9 minutes. Let cool on baking sheets on a cooling rack. Repeat with remaining cookies.

5. Assemble sandwiches: Spread jam onto bottom of half the cookies, then top with remaining cookies.

PER SERVING

About 280 calories, 14 g fat (9 g saturated fat), 3 g protein, 335 mg sodium, 38 g carbohydrates, 1 g fiber

≡ INGREDIENT ≡
SPOTLIGHT

Cake Flour

Cake flour has a lower protein content than all-purpose flour, so it's ideal for making tender cookies. Don't have cake flour? For every cup of cake flour required, add 2 tablespoons cornstarch to a 1-cup measure. Spoon all-purpose flour to fill the cup, and then level it off.

GIFT IT!

Line a berry basket with polka-dot tissue paper
and add cookies. Wrap with rickrack ribbon and sew
in place with a button and embroidery thread.

Cookie Shooters

Why, yes, those are milk and cookies rolled into one sweet work of art! With the help of a popover pan, you can make your own chocolate chip beauties to fill with whatever your heart desires.

Active Time 25 minutes | **Total Time** 1 hour, plus chilling | **Makes** 12

3⅓ cups all-purpose flour

⅓ cup cornstarch

1½ teaspoons baking powder

1¼ teaspoons baking soda

1¼ teaspoons salt

1¼ cups (2½ sticks) unsalted butter, at room temperature

1½ cups packed brown sugar

¾ cup granulated sugar

2 large eggs

1 tablespoon pure vanilla extract

1 12-ounce package mini semisweet chocolate chips

⅓ cup chocolate chips or chunks, melted

Milk, chocolate liqueur or coffee liqueur of choice, for serving

1. In a large bowl, whisk together flour, cornstarch, baking powder, baking soda and salt; set aside.

2. Using an electric mixer, beat butter and sugars in a large bowl on medium-high speed until fluffy, about 5 minutes. Add eggs one at a time, beating well after each addition. Beat in vanilla. Reduce speed to low, add flour mixture and mix until just combined. Add mini chocolate chips and mix until evenly distributed. Refrigerate dough until firm.

3. Heat oven to 350°F. Break off a golf-ball-size piece of dough; roll into a ball (should be about 1½ inches wide) and place into one cup of a nonstick popover pan. Repeat for the remaining 5 cups. Using the rounded end of a wooden spoon and your fingertips, press dough into the center and then up the side of the cup to form a very thin, even layer of dough. Patch up any tears with bits of extra dough. Repeat with remaining dough.

4. Bake 8 minutes, then use the end of the same wooden spoon to gently press dough down and against the side of the pan to deflate. Bake another 2 minutes, then repeat pressing to deflate. Bake until golden brown and crisp around edges, 2 more minutes. Transfer the pan to a wire rack and press to deflate once more.

5. Using a small offset spatula, gently loosen sides of cookies from the pan. Let cool for 10 minutes in the pan. Loosen sides of cookies again. Place a cooling rack on top of the pan. Holding the rack against the pan, invert cups onto rack. Let cool completely. Repeat this process once more with remaining dough and cooled popover pan. (You will have dough left over, which you can refrigerate for up to 3 days or freeze for up to a month for another use.)

6. With a small pastry brush, paint insides of cookies with a thick layer of melted chocolate. Let sit until chocolate is set, 1 hour. Serve filled with milk, chocolate liqueur or coffee liqueur. Once filled, serve within 5 minutes. Store unfilled cookies in an airtight container at room temperature for up to 3 days.

PER SERVING

About 210 calories, 10 g fat (6 g saturated fat), 2 g protein, 145 mg sodium, 30 g carbohydrates, 1 g fiber

TEST
KITCHEN
TIP

Wait to add the milk,
liqueur or any other liquid
until just before serving.
Otherwise, the cookie
shooters will become
a soggy mess.

Homemade Fudgy Ice Cream Sandwiches

These decadent cookies stay chewy even when frozen, so they're ideal for ice cream sandwiches.

Active Time 10 minutes | **Total Time** 20 minutes, plus cooling and freezing | **Makes** 12

½ cup (1 stick) unsalted butter, at room temperature

1 12-ounce package semisweet chocolate chips

1 14-ounce can sweetened condensed milk

¼ teaspoon kosher salt

1 cup all-purpose flour

1 tablespoon pure vanilla extract

Ice cream, slightly softened, for serving

1. Heat oven to 350°F. Line 2 baking sheets with parchment paper.

2. In a 4-quart saucepan, combine butter, chocolate chips, sweetened condensed milk and salt. Cook on medium-low until melted, 5 to 6 minutes, stirring. Remove from heat. Stir in flour and vanilla until combined.

3. With a 1½-inch-wide cookie scoop, scoop mounds of dough onto the prepared sheets, spacing them 2 inches apart. Use your hands to flatten slightly. Bake until the tops are dry but still soft when pressed, 8 to 10 minutes. Let cool on baking sheets on a cooling rack for 5 minutes before transferring to the rack to cool completely.

4. Assemble sandwiches: Press 1 small scoop ice cream between 2 cookies. Freeze until ready to serve.

PER SERVING

About 420 calories, 23 g fat (14 g saturated fat), 6 g protein, 115 mg sodium, 52 g carbohydrates, 2 g fiber

TEST
KITCHEN
TIP

These cookies also taste incredible on their own — sans ice cream! Just bake an extra minute or two, then store in airtight containers.

Snickerdoodle Ice Cream Sandwiches

Brown sugar, pure vanilla extract and ground cinnamon give this soft cookie just the right amount of spice. Paired with the ice cream of your choosing — vanilla, mint chocolate chip, strawberry, you name it — it's summertime sweetness at its finest.

Active Time 25 minutes | **Total Time** 1 hour 25 minutes | **Makes** 12

1½ cups all-purpose flour

1 teaspoon cream of tartar

½ teaspoon baking soda

¼ teaspoon kosher salt

½ cup (1 stick) unsalted butter, at room temperature

½ cup plus 2 tablespoons firmly packed light brown sugar

4 tablespoons granulated sugar

1 large egg

1 teaspoon pure vanilla extract

¾ teaspoon ground cinnamon

3 cups ice cream

Cookie Cheat!

For an instant dessert, press a scoop of ice cream between two store-bought cookies. Try one of these flavor combos:

· **Chocolate Sandwich Cookies** + **Cookies-and-Cream Ice Cream**

· **Stroopwafels** + **Blood Orange Sorbet**

· **Pink Wafer Cookies** + **Vanilla Ice Cream**

· **Ginger Cookies** + **Blueberry Ice Cream**

· **Biscoff Cookies** + **Belgian Chocolate Ice Cream**

· **Chocolate Wafer Cookies** + **Mint Chocolate Chip Ice Cream**

1. Heat oven to 350°F. Line 2 baking sheets with parchment paper.

2. In a medium bowl, whisk together flour, cream of tartar, baking soda and salt; set aside.

3. Using an electric mixer, beat butter, brown sugar and 2 tablespoons granulated sugar in a large bowl on medium speed until light and fluffy, about 3 minutes. Beat in egg and vanilla. Reduce speed to low and gradually add flour mixture, mixing until just incorporated.

4. In a small bowl, combine cinnamon and remaining 2 tablespoons granulated sugar. Form the dough into 1½-inch balls, roll in cinnamon-sugar mixture and place onto the prepared sheets, spacing them 2 inches apart. Bake until set and slightly golden brown around edges, 10 to 12 minutes. Let cool on baking sheets for 5 minutes before transferring to a cooling rack to cool completely.

5. Assemble sandwiches: Press ¼ cup ice cream between 2 cookies. Serve immediately or freeze, covered, for up to 3 days.

PER SERVING

About 270 calories, 13 g fat (8 g saturated fat), 4 g protein, 120 mg sodium, 36 g carbohydrates, 1 g fiber

Chocolate Chip Triple-Decker Cake

Who needs cake? Featuring layers of ice cream, gigantic chocolate chip cookies and a rich chocolate sauce, this impressive dessert can easily steal the show. (See photo, page 148.)

Active Time 1 hour | **Total Time** 1 hour, plus chilling and freezing | **Makes** 1 (serves 16)

4 cups all-purpose flour

4 teaspoons cornstarch

1 teaspoon baking soda

1 teaspoon kosher salt

1½ cups (3 sticks) unsalted butter, melted and slightly cooled

1½ cups packed dark brown sugar

½ cup granulated sugar

2 large eggs, plus 2 large egg yolks

4 teaspoons pure vanilla extract

3 cups bittersweet chocolate chips

1½ pints vanilla chocolate-chip ice cream, softened

1½ pints mint chip ice cream, softened

1½ pints chocolate chocolate-chip ice cream, softened

Chocolate sauce, for serving

1. Line 2 large baking sheets with parchment paper. In a large bowl, whisk together flour, cornstarch, baking soda and salt; set aside.

2. Using an electric mixer, beat butter and sugars in a large bowl on medium speed until combined, about 1 to 2 minutes. Beat in eggs, egg yolks and vanilla. Reduce speed to low and slowly add flour mixture until just combined. Fold in chocolate chips.

3. Divide cookie dough into 4 equal portions. Press into four 6-inch disks; place 2 disks onto each prepared sheet. Refrigerate for 4 hours or up to 2 days.

4. Heat oven to 325°F. Bake, rotating the positions of the baking sheets halfway through, until golden brown around edges but centers are still soft, 20 to 24 minutes. Let cool completely on baking sheets on a cooling rack.

5. Top 3 cookies with one flavor of ice cream each, spreading to edges; freeze for at least 4 hours or up to 24 hours. Stack frozen cookies on a cake plate or platter and top with remaining cookie.

6. Freeze until ready to serve. Let sit at room temperature before cutting, 10 to 15 minutes. Top with chocolate sauce just before serving.

PER SERVING
About 940 calories, 52 g fat (32 g saturated fat), 12 g protein, 315 mg sodium, 108 g carbohydrates, 6 g fiber

TEST KITCHEN TIP

Once frozen, let this cookies-and-cream cake sit at room temperature for 10 to 15 minutes before slicing. When it's time to slice, use a large chef's knife warmed under hot tap water.

Skillet S'mores

No campfire? No problem! These campfire-inspired skillet cookies get their signature char from the broiler.

Active Time 25 minutes | **Total Time** 1 hour | **Makes** 12

⅓ cup all-purpose flour, plus more for the surface

⅓ cup graham or whole-wheat flour

1 teaspoon ground cinnamon

½ teaspoon kosher salt

¼ teaspoon baking soda

3 tablespoons unsalted butter, at room temperature

⅓ cup packed light brown sugar

1 large egg

2 teaspoons honey

½ teaspoon pure vanilla extract

1½ cups semisweet chocolate chips

6 s'more marshmallows (such as S'more Mallows)

TEST KITCHEN TIP

Have leftover chocolate chip cookies? Let this recipe inspire you to turn them into quick skillet treats: Just jump to Step 3 and use whatever leftover chocolate chip cookies you have on hand. (Adjust other amounts accordingly.)

1. Heat oven to 350°F with the racks in the middle and top thirds. Line 2 baking sheets with parchment paper. In a medium bowl, whisk together flours, cinnamon, salt and baking soda; set aside.

2. Using an electric mixer, beat butter and sugar in a large bowl on medium speed until light and fluffy, 1 to 2 minutes. Beat in egg, honey and vanilla until combined. Reduce speed to low and slowly add in flour mixture, mixing until incorporated. Scoop mounds of dough (1½ tablespoons each) onto the prepared sheets, spacing them 2 inches apart. Bake, one sheet at a time on the middle rack, until golden brown around edges, 9 to 10 minutes. Let cool on baking sheets on a cooling rack for 5 minutes before transferring cookies to the rack to cool completely.

3. Place twelve 3.5-inch cast-iron skillets (or one 9-inch cast-iron skillet) on a rimmed baking sheet. Fill with chocolate chips, dividing evenly. Top with cookies. Use a serrated knife to cut marshmallows in half crosswise; use a 2-inch star-shaped cookie cutter to cut into shapes (discard excess marshmallow). Top cookies with marshmallow stars. Bake on the top rack until chocolate is melted, 4 to 5 minutes. Switch oven to broil. Broil until marshmallows are golden brown, about 30 seconds. Serve immediately.

PER SERVING

About 210 calories, 10 g fat (6 g saturated fat), 2 g protein, 125 mg sodium, 32 g carbohydrates, 2 g fiber

Skillet Cookie Sundaes

The beauty of a skillet cookie is that it's baked in (and eaten from!) the pan, so you can get right to it — no scooping, rolling or cutting needed. Serve it warm with ice cream or try one of the homemade toppings on the opposite page.

Active Time 25 minutes | **Total Time** 50 minutes | **Makes** 8

For the Graham Cracker Layer

- 6 tablespoons unsalted butter, melted and cooled
- ¼ cup granulated sugar
- 1½ cups graham cracker crumbs (from 12 sheets)
- ¾ cup semisweet chocolate chips

For the Cookie Dough Layer

- 1 cup loosely packed dark brown sugar
- ¾ cup (1½ sticks) unsalted butter, melted and cooled
- 1 tablespoon pure vanilla extract
- 1 large egg plus 1 egg yolk
- 1½ cups all-purpose flour
- ¾ teaspoon baking powder
- ½ teaspoon kosher salt
- ½ cup sweetened shredded coconut
- ⅓ cup semisweet chocolate chips
- Ice cream, for serving

1. Heat oven to 350°F. Make the graham cracker layer: In a medium bowl, combine melted butter and granulated sugar. Stir in graham cracker crumbs until moistened. Press mixture into the bottom of a 10-inch cast-iron skillet or eight 5-inch mini skillets. Sprinkle chocolate chips evenly over graham cracker crust.

2. Make the cookie dough layer: In a large bowl, whisk together brown sugar and melted butter. Add vanilla, egg and egg yolk, and whisk until combined. Add flour, baking powder and salt, and mix until fully combined. Stir in coconut and chocolate chips.

3. Spread cookie dough evenly over graham cracker crust. Bake until just slightly gooey in the middle but golden brown around edges, 25 to 30 minutes.

4. Remove from the oven and let cool slightly, until the pan is cool to the touch. Serve with assorted ice creams and toppings, at right, if desired.

PER SERVING

About 650 calories, 38 g fat (23 g saturated fat), 6 g protein, 295 mg sodium, 74 g carbohydrates, 3 g fiber

TEST KITCHEN TIP

To make graham cracker crumbs, place cookies in a heavy-duty resealable plastic bag and crush them with a rolling pin or meat mallet; you can also use a food processor or blender.

Bonus Topping Recipes!

Take these skillet cookies to the next level with a few homemade accompaniments to serve alongside — including candied nuts, caramel sauce and roasted fruit.

Sweet & Spicy Candied Pecans

In a large heavy skillet on medium, cook **2 cups pecans**, **1 cup sugar** and **1/3 cup water**, stirring frequently, until bubbling, 2 to 3 minutes. Continue cooking and stirring until liquid evaporates and sugar crystallizes (nuts will look sandy), 5 to 7 minutes. Reduce heat to medium-low and cook, stirring constantly, until sugar becomes golden and syrupy, 8 to 10 minutes. Remove the skillet from heat and immediately stir in **1/4 teaspoon ground cinnamon**, **pinch chili powder**, **pinch cayenne** and **1/4 teaspoon kosher salt**. Quickly spread nuts onto a parchment-lined baking sheet. Let cool completely before breaking into clumps.

Miso Caramel

In a small saucepan on medium-low, combine **3/4 cup heavy cream** and **6 tablespoons unsalted butter**, stirring, until melted. Whisk in **3 tablespoons white miso paste** and **3/4 cup packed dark brown sugar**, whisking, until slightly thickened and mixture coats the back of a spoon, 6 to 8 minutes. Use right away or refrigerate and rewarm before serving. Makes 2/3 cup.

Maple-Roasted Strawberries

In a large bowl, whisk **2 tablespoons maple syrup**, **1 tablespoon olive oil**, **2 teaspoons balsamic vinegar** and **1/4 teaspoon kosher salt**. Fold in **1 pound strawberries** (hulled and halved). Transfer to a parchment-lined baking sheet, arrange in a single layer and roast at 350°F until juices are thickened, 40 to 45 minutes.

Mini Meringues

Switching up the flavors and colors of these light and airy egg-white kisses is easy: Just add extracts and food coloring to the batter.

Active Time 20 minutes | **Total Time** 2 hours 25 minutes | **Makes** 60

3   large egg whites

Pinch kosher salt

¼   teaspoon cream of tartar

½   cup sugar

½   teaspoon pure vanilla extract

Assorted food coloring pastes

Switch It Up!

Choose a color and add a "matching" flavor in Steps 2 and 3:

- **½ teaspoon almond extract ◆ green**
- **2 teaspoons freshly grated lemon zest ◆ yellow**
- **½ teaspoon mint extract ◆ red**
- **¼ cup freeze-dried blueberries, finely crushed ◆ purple**

INGREDIENT SPOTLIGHT
Cream of Tartar

Whether you're whipping up egg whites for meringues or making Royal Icing, adding a pinch of this baking staple helps to stabilize whatever is in your mixer.

1. Heat oven to 225°F with the racks in the top and bottom thirds. Line 2 large baking sheets with parchment paper.

2. Using an electric mixer, beat egg whites and salt in a medium bowl on medium speed until foamy, about 5 to 7 minutes. Add cream of tartar; beat on medium-high until soft peaks form. Add sugar 1 tablespoon at a time. Beat until meringue stands in stiff, glossy peaks, 5 to 7 minutes more. Beat in vanilla and a flavor, if using (see "Switch It Up!" at left).

3. For each color desired, use a small brush to lightly paint 3 or 4 stripes of food coloring inside a large piping bag fitted with a ½-inch plain tip. Divide meringue among the piping bags. Pipe meringue into 1½-inch rounds onto the prepared sheets, spacing them 1 inch apart.

4. Bake 1 hour. Turn off the oven; let sit in the oven for 1 hour with door closed. Remove from the oven; let cool completely on the baking sheets. Cookies can be stored in airtight containers at room temperature for up to 2 weeks.

PER SERVING

About 5 calories, 0 g fat (0 g saturated fat), 0 g protein, 10 mg sodium, 2 g carbohydrates, 0 g fiber

Peanut Butter Balls

This no-bake classic, also known as buckeyes, just may be the easiest, most delicious treat you can bring to your cookie swap.

Active Time 30 minutes | **Total Time** 55 minutes | **Makes** 32

2 cups confectioners' sugar

1 cup creamy peanut butter

4 tablespoons unsalted butter, at room temperature

1 teaspoon pure vanilla extract

¼ teaspoon kosher salt

9 ounces bittersweet chocolate, chopped

Flaky sea salt and melted red candy melts, for decorating

Cookie Cheat!

Here's a quick way to round out the cookie tray: Start with a store-bought shortcut, then "baking" is a breeze.

Chocolate-Dipped Madeleines

Partially dip **store-bought madeleine cookies** into **melted white chocolate** on a diagonal and then transfer to a parchment-lined baking sheet. Sprinkle with **crushed freeze-dried raspberries** and let set.

Waffle Sandwich Cookies

Using an electric mixer, beat **8 ounces cream cheese** (at room temperature), **4 tablespoons unsalted butter** (at room temperature), **6 tablespoons confectioners' sugar** and **2 teaspoons orange zest** until light and fluffy, 2 to 3 minutes. Spread **12 Belgian butter waffle cookies** with 2 tablespoons each of the cream cheese mixture, then sandwich with 12 more cookies. Serve immediately.

1. Using an electric mixer, beat sugar, peanut butter, butter, vanilla and salt in a large bowl on medium speed until dough forms into a ball, about 2 minutes.

2. Line 2 baking sheets with parchment paper. Roll dough into 1-inch balls and place onto one of the prepared sheets. Freeze until firm, about 20 minutes.

3. Once balls are firm, place chocolate in a small measuring cup and microwave in 30-second increments, stirring between each, until melted and smooth.

4. Working with a fourth of the balls at a time (keep remaining frozen), dip into chocolate one at a time, letting excess drip off, and then place onto the other prepared sheet. Sprinkle with flaky salt if desired. Repeat with remaining peanut butter balls.

5. Once chocolate has set, decorate with melted red candy melts if desired. Keep refrigerated until ready to serve.

PER SERVING
About 130 calories, 9 g fat (3.5 g saturated fat), 3 g protein, 50 mg sodium, 13 g carbohydrates, 1 g fiber

GIFT IT!
Line a gift box with tissue paper, then place balls into matching mini cupcake liners.

Walnut Biscotti

Biscotti is derived from the Latin *biscoctus*, meaning "twice baked," which best describes the signature baking method that results in a sweet that is sturdy enough to be shipped across the country *and* strong enough to be dunked into a cup of hot coffee.

Active Time 40 minutes | **Total Time** 1 hour 40 minutes, plus cooling | **Makes** 36

2	cups all-purpose flour
1½	teaspoons baking powder
¼	teaspoon kosher salt
½	cup (1 stick) unsalted butter, at room temperature
⅓	cup granulated sugar
⅓	cup packed brown sugar
2	large eggs
1	tablespoon pure vanilla extract
1	cup walnuts, toasted and chopped
12	ounces white chocolate, melted, optional

Cookie Cheat!

Easily upgrade **store-bought biscotti** by dipping them into **melted white or dark chocolate**, then placing on a parchment-lined baking sheet and refrigerating until chocolate is set, about 15 minutes.

1. Heat oven to 325°F. Line a large baking sheet with parchment paper. In a medium bowl, combine flour, baking powder and salt; set aside.

2. Using an electric mixer, beat butter and sugars in a large bowl on medium speed until light and fluffy, about 3 minutes. Add eggs, one at a time, beating well after each addition. Add in vanilla. Reduce speed to low; gradually mix in flour mixture until just incorporated. Stir in walnuts.

3. Divide dough in half. Form each half into a log, 1½ inches wide, on the prepared sheet, spacing them 3 inches apart.

4. Bake until golden brown, 30 minutes. Let cool on baking sheet on a cooling rack for 5 minutes.

5. Slide the logs onto a cutting board. With a serrated knife, cut each log crosswise into ½-inch-thick diagonal slices; place, cut side down, on the same sheet. Bake until golden brown and crisp, 20 to 25 minutes. Let cool completely on baking sheet on a cooling rack.

6. Dip half of each cookie into chocolate if desired. Let set on parchment paper. Store in airtight containers (layered with parchment paper if dipped) at room temperature for up to a week or in the freezer for up to a month.

PER SERVING

About 90 calories, 5 g fat (2 g saturated fat), 2 g protein, 45 mg sodium, 10 g carbohydrates, 0 g fiber

Apricot & Pistachio Cornmeal Biscotti

For extra crunchy biscotti, reach for cornmeal. This versatile pantry staple is good for so much more than just cornbread. Then, fold salted pistachios (or whatever nut you choose!) and dried apricots into the dough.

Active Time 35 minutes | **Total Time** 1 hour 20 minutes | **Makes** 84

2 cups all-purpose flour

½ cup cornmeal

½ teaspoon baking powder

½ teaspoon kosher salt

4 tablespoons canola oil

1 cup sugar

2 large eggs

2 teaspoons pure vanilla extract

2 teaspoons orange zest

1 cup shelled pistachios

1 cup dried apricots, thinly sliced

1. Heat oven to 350°F. Line 2 baking sheets with parchment paper. In a medium bowl, whisk together flour, cornmeal, baking powder and salt; set aside.

2. Using an electric mixer, beat oil, sugar, eggs, vanilla and orange zest in a large bowl on medium speed until combined, about 2 minutes. Gradually add flour mixture, mixing until fully incorporated (dough will be very stiff). Fold in pistachios and apricots.

3. Divide dough into 6 equal portions and, with floured hands, roll each portion into a 1½- by 6-inch log. Place crosswise onto the prepared sheets and slightly flatten the tops.

4. Bake, rotating the positions of the baking sheets halfway through, until light golden brown and beginning to crack on top, 30 to 40 minutes. Let cool on baking sheets for 15 minutes.

5. Using a serrated knife, cut logs on a slight diagonal into ¼-inch-thick slices. Arrange slices on the same baking sheets in a single layer and bake until lightly golden brown, 10 to 12 minutes more. Transfer to a cooling rack to cool completely.

PER SERVING
About 45 calories, 1 g fat (0 g saturated fat), 1 g protein, 20 mg sodium, 7 g carbohydrates, 0 g fiber

Chapter 6

Let's Celebrate!

Now that you've mastered the basics (and beyond!), it's time to find excuses to bake cookies as often as possible. Enter: holidays and occasions of all sizes. From confections for springtime celebrations to spooky Halloween options, this chapter has 61 reasons to turn on the oven. Plus, the ultimate Christmas cookie countdown (page 242) also features 25 ways to transform sugar cookie dough.

REINDEER & TREE COOKIES 234

←

Fancy Fortunes

Celebrate any occasion — an anniversary, a birthday, New Year's, you name it! — with this homemade version of fortune cookies. You can fill the cookies with customized, handwritten messages ranging from "Thanks for being a friend!" to "Will you marry me?" The choice is yours!

Active Time 10 minutes | **Total Time** 40 minutes, plus cooling | **Makes** 10

2	tablespoons (¼ stick) unsalted butter
¼	cup confectioners' sugar
1	large egg white
1	teaspoon pure vanilla extract
⅛	teaspoon kosher salt
¼	cup all-purpose flour
10	strips paper (3 inches by ½ inch) with fortunes
	Melted dark, milk or white chocolate and chopped nuts for decorating, optional

Cookie Cheat!

Dunk store-bought fortune cookies into **melted chocolate**, then roll in **nuts** or drizzle with more melted chocolate.

1. Heat oven to 375°F. Line 2 small baking sheets with parchment paper.

2. In a small saucepan, heat butter on low until melted; remove from heat. Whisk in confectioners' sugar, egg white, vanilla and salt to combine. Mix in flour until smooth.

3. Drop heaping teaspoonfuls of batter onto the prepared sheets, spacing them at least 4 inches apart. With a small offset spatula or the back of a spoon, spread batter evenly to form 3-inch rounds.

4. Bake until light golden brown, 6 to 7 minutes. Loosen cookies with a metal spatula; flip onto flat sides.

5. Working with one cookie at a time, place fortune across center of hot cookie, then fold in half to form a semicircle; press edges together.

6. Quickly fold the semicircle over the edge of a small bowl to create a fortune-cookie shape. Place in a mini muffin pan to hold the shape. Repeat with remaining cookies.

7. Repeat with remaining batter and fortunes, cooling the baking sheets between batches.

8. If desired, dip cookies into chocolate (or drizzle them), then roll in nuts. Place on parchment paper until set.

PER SERVING

About 50 calories, 3 g fat (2 g saturated fat), 1 g protein, 50 mg sodium, 6 g carbohydrates, 0 g fiber

Best year yet!

Chinese Almond Cookies

These treats resemble coins and are a symbol of good fortune during the Lunar New Year. They are made with lard instead of butter, which helps to create a sandier texture. Toasting the almonds in this recipe deepens the almond flavor of the dough.

Active Time 40 minutes | **Total Time** 1 hour 5 minutes | **Makes** 18

2/3 cup whole almonds (about 4 ounces)

1 cup all-purpose flour

3/4 cup confectioners' sugar

1 teaspoon baking powder

1 teaspoon baking soda

1/2 teaspoon kosher salt

4 egg yolks, at room temperature

2/3 cup melted lard, cooled until barely warm

1 1/2 teaspoons pure almond extract

1. Heat oven to 350°F. On a small rimmed baking sheet, roast almonds until fragrant and beginning to brown, about 10 minutes. Let cool completely. Reserve 18 almonds for topping cookies.

2. Place remaining cooled almonds in a food processor along with flour, confectioners' sugar, baking powder, baking soda and salt, and pulse until almonds are very finely ground, about 30 seconds; transfer to a medium bowl.

3. In a small bowl, whisk together 2 egg yolks, lard and almond extract. Add to the bowl with flour mixture, stirring until flour is incorporated and dough just comes together (do not overmix). Cover with plastic wrap, pressing to adhere to surface, and let dough rest, 20 minutes.

4. Line 2 baking sheets with parchment paper. Roll dough into 1 1/4-inch balls and place onto the prepared sheets, spacing them 3 inches apart. Flatten balls to about 1/3 inch thick, molding any cracked edges slightly with fingers.

5. In a small bowl, whisk together remaining 2 egg yolks. Generously brush tops and edges of cookies with yolk. Press a reserved almond into center of each cookie and then bake, rotating the positions of the baking sheets halfway through, until golden brown on bottom and just beginning to turn golden brown on sides, 14 to 18 minutes. (Cookies will feel set when lightly touched but will still be soft at this point. They harden as they cool.) Let cool on baking sheets for 2 minutes before transferring to a cooling rack to cool completely.

PER SERVING

About 160 calories, 11 g fat (4 g saturated fat), 2 g protein, 155 mg sodium, 12 g carbohydrates, 1 g fiber

Sweetheart Cookies

With a heart-shaped cookie cutter and some luster dust, a batch of sugar cookie dough can easily turn into a simple, delicious sweet that practically screams "baked with love."

Active Time 10 minutes | **Total Time** 45 minutes, plus cooling | **Makes** 36 to 48 (depending on size and shape)

1 batch Classic Sugar Cookie Dough (page 18)

1 batch Royal Icing (page 24)

Luster dust and vodka, for decorating

1. Prepare cookies per recipe instructions, using floured heart-shaped cookie cutters to cut out shapes. Let cool completely before decorating.

2. Ice cookies with the Royal Icing and let set. When ready to decorate, combine luster dust with a touch of vodka and use a clean small brush to paint on stripes.

PER SERVING

About 130 calories, 5 g fat (3 g saturated fat), 1 g protein, 35 mg sodium, 21 g carbohydrates, 0 g fiber

INGREDIENT SPOTLIGHT

Luster Dust

This edible powder adds color and sparkle to desserts. To brush it onto baked goods, mix the powder with an alcohol-based liquid such as vodka or flavored extract.

Jammin' Heart Cookies

Similar to conversation hearts, these linzer torte cookies spell out messages of love. Bake a batch to give to your valentine — they're even better than a box of chocolates!

Active Time 40 minutes | **Total Time** 1 hour, plus chilling and cooling | **Makes** 30

¾   cup pecans

1½   cups all-purpose flour

½   teaspoon ground cinnamon

     Pinch ground cloves

     Pinch ground allspice

¼   teaspoon kosher salt

½   cup (1 stick) unsalted butter, at room temperature

½   cup granulated sugar

1   large egg

1   12-ounce jar cherry jam

     Confectioners' sugar, for dusting

1. In a food processor, pulse pecans and 2 tablespoons flour to form fine crumbs. Add cinnamon, cloves, allspice, salt and remaining flour, and pulse to combine; set aside.

2. Using an electric mixer, beat butter and sugar in a large bowl on medium-high speed until light and fluffy, about 3 minutes. Beat in egg. Reduce speed to low and mix in pecan-flour mixture until just combined.

3. Divide dough in half. Roll each half between 2 sheets of parchment paper to ⅛ inch thick, then freeze until firm, about 30 minutes.

4. Heat oven to 350°F. Line 2 baking sheets with parchment paper. Working with one sheet of dough at a time, use a 2-inch round fluted cutter to cut out cookies; transfer to the prepared sheets, spacing them 2 inches apart. Reroll, chill and cut scraps.

5. Use small ½- to 1-inch letter and heart cookie cutters to cut out shapes from centers of half the cookies. Bake until light golden brown around edges, 12 to 16 minutes. Let cool completely on baking sheets.

6. Using a wire-mesh strainer, pass jam through and discard any large cherry pieces. Spoon 1 teaspoon strained jam onto each whole cookie. Dust cutout cookies with confectioners' sugar and place over jam to create sandwiches.

PER SERVING

About 110 calories, 5 g fat (2 g saturated fat), 1 g protein, 20 mg sodium, 16 g carbohydrates, 0 g fiber

Hamantaschen

These treats are a staple of the Jewish holiday Purim. To shape them into the traditional triangles, cut circles from thinly rolled dough, add a spoonful of filling and then fold in the sides, pinching the three points.

Active Time 1 hour | **Total Time** 1 hour 55 minutes | **Makes** 32

For the Dough

2 ½   cups all-purpose flour

¾   teaspoon baking powder

¼   teaspoon salt

½   cup (1 stick) unsalted butter, at room temperature

½   cup granulated sugar

1   large egg

3   tablespoons lemon juice plus 1 teaspoon lemon zest

1   teaspoon pure vanilla extract

For the Filling

½   pound apricots or prunes

1   tablespoon fresh lemon juice

1   tablespoon granulated sugar

1. Prepare the dough: In a bowl, whisk together flour, baking powder and salt; set aside.

2. Using an electric mixer, beat butter and sugar in a large bowl on medium-high until light and fluffy, 3 minutes. Reduce speed to medium and mix in egg until fully incorporated, then lemon juice, zest and vanilla.

3. Reduce speed to low and gradually mix in flour. Dough will be soft. Divide in half and roll each between 2 sheets of parchment to about ⅛ inch thick. Refrigerate until firm, about 30 minutes.

4. Meanwhile, prepare the filling: Place apricots or prunes in a small saucepan. Add lemon juice and sugar. Cover with water (about 1 cup) and bring to a boil. Reduce heat and simmer until fruit is plump and nearly all the liquid has evaporated, about 20 minutes. Transfer mixture to a food processor and purée until smooth.

5. Heat oven to 375°F. Line 2 baking sheets with parchment paper. Using a 3-inch round cookie cutter, cut out rounds. Reroll, chill and cut scraps.

6. To assemble cookies, place 1 teaspoon filling in the center of each round. To make triangular pocket, fold in two "sides" and pinch top corner to seal. Fold third side up to meet the other sides and pinch corners to seal, leaving a small opening in the center. Transfer to the prepared sheets, spacing them 1 inch apart.

7. Bake, one sheet at a time, until golden brown, 12 to 13 minutes. Let cool on baking sheets for 2 minutes before transferring to a cooling rack to cool completely. Repeat with remaining dough and filling.

PER SERVING

About 95 calories, 3 g fat (2 g saturated fat), 1 g protein, 30 mg sodium, 16 g carbohydrates, 1 g fiber

Nan-e Berenji

Celebrate the start of spring and Nowruz (Persian New Year) by baking up a batch of these delicate rice cookies flavored with rosewater and cardamom.

Active Time 1 hour | **Total Time** 2 hours 5 minutes | **Makes** 30

1½ cups rice flour, preferably stone ground

½ teaspoon kosher salt

½ cup (1 stick) unsalted butter, at room temperature

⅔ cup confectioners' sugar

½ teaspoon ground cardamom

1 egg yolk, at room temperature

1½ tablespoons rosewater

1 tablespoon milk

1 teaspoon poppy seeds

TEST KITCHEN TIP

Many use a traditional cookie stamp to make the spiral indentations on the top, but you can achieve a similar effect using the side of a spoon.

1. In a small bowl, whisk together rice flour and salt; set aside.

2. In a food processor, combine butter, confectioners' sugar and cardamom. Process until fully combined and lightened in color, scraping down side as necessary, 1 to 2 minutes. Add egg yolk, rosewater and milk, and pulse, scraping down side as necessary, until fully incorporated. Add rice flour mixture and pulse until a smooth dough has formed.

3. Transfer dough to a piece of plastic wrap and use wrap to form into a 1-inch-thick disk. Wrap well and refrigerate until slightly firm but not hard, about 45 minutes.

4. Heat oven to 300°F. Line 2 baking sheets with parchment paper. Remove dough from the refrigerator and divide in half; cover one half and return to the refrigerator. Roll the other half into 1-inch balls and place onto the prepared sheets, spacing them 2 inches apart. Flatten balls to ½ inch thick and use the side of a small spoon to make indentations in each cookie (approximately ⅛ inch deep), forming a pinwheel pattern.

5. Sprinkle with poppy seeds and bake, rotating the positions of the baking sheets halfway through, until just beginning to turn golden brown on bottom, 20 to 22 minutes. Transfer to a cooling rack and let cool. Repeat with remaining dough and poppy seeds.

PER SERVING

About 70 calories, 3 g fat (2 g saturated fat), 1 g protein, 30 mg sodium, 10 g carbohydrates, 0 g fiber

Chocolate Stout Whoopie Pies

The whoopie pie is rumored to be named for the excited cheers of children who found these in their lunchboxes. Stout beer folded into the chocolate cake batter adds complexity and depth — and turns the childhood favorite into a perfect grown-up St. Patrick's Day treat.

Active Time 30 minutes | **Total Time** 50 minutes | **Makes** 15

For the Whoopie Pies

- 1 cup all-purpose flour
- ¼ cup unsweetened cocoa powder
- ¾ teaspoon baking soda
- ¼ teaspoon baking powder
- ¼ teaspoon kosher salt
- ½ cup packed light brown sugar
- ¼ cup (½ stick) unsalted butter, at room temperature
- 1 large egg
- ⅓ cup 2 percent low-fat milk
- ¼ cup stout beer (such as Guinness)

For the Filling

- 2 ounces cream cheese, at room temperature
- ¼ cup confectioners' sugar, sifted
- ½ cup marshmallow cream

1. Heat oven to 375°F. Line 2 baking sheets with parchment paper. In a medium bowl, whisk together flour, cocoa powder, baking soda, baking powder and salt; set aside.

2. Using an electric mixer, beat brown sugar and butter in a large bowl on medium speed until light and fluffy, about 3 minutes. Beat in egg. Alternately add flour mixture and milk to the mixture, then add stout and mix until just incorporated.

3. Drop level tablespoonfuls of dough onto the prepared sheets, spacing them 2 inches apart. Bake until tops are set and spring back when lightly pressed, 6 to 8 minutes. Let cool on baking sheets for 5 minutes before transferring to a cooling rack to cool completely.

4. While cookies cool, make the filling: Using an electric mixer, beat cream cheese in a medium bowl on medium-high speed until smooth, about 3 minutes. Add confectioners' sugar and beat until fluffy. Fold in marshmallow cream and beat until fluffy, about 3 minutes. Cover and refrigerate for at least 20 minutes before using.

5. When ready to serve, assemble sandwiches: Spread filling onto half the cookies, then top with remaining cookies.

PER SERVING
About 130 calories, 5 g fat (3 g saturated fat),
2 g protein, 130 mg sodium, 20 g carbohydrates, 1 g fiber

TEST
KITCHEN
TIP

Use white gel icing to
add football laces to these
chocolate-and-cream
sandwiches for a
tailgating treat.

Easter Egg Cookies

Dyeing eggs may be tradition, but decorating egg-shaped cookies with pastel icings and fun festive sprinkles doubles as dessert. Sugar cookies are the ultimate blank canvas: Start by baking a batch of cookies using the Classic Sugar Cookie Dough (page 18) and an egg-shaped cutter. Then get to decorating!

1

Marbled Egg Sugar Cookies

Active Time 25 minutes
Total Time 40 minutes
Makes 36 to 48 (depending on size and shape)

- 1 batch Classic Sugar Cookie Dough (page 18)
- 1 batch Royal Icing (page 24)
  Gel food coloring

1. Prepare cookies per recipe instructions, using floured egg-shaped cookie cutters to cut out shapes. Let cool completely before decorating.

2. While cookies cool, prepare the Royal Icing through Step 2. Add water 1 teaspoon at a time to make a thin drizzling consistency. Spoon 3 tablespoons onto a plate. Add a bit of food coloring and use a toothpick to swirl the color.

3. Place a cookie top down directly into icing, then slowly peel cookie away to one side, turning upright and letting excess fall off. Transfer to a cooling rack to set. Repeat with remaining cookies, changing icing colors as desired.

PER SERVING

About 110 calories, 4 g fat (2.5 g saturated fat), 1 g protein, 20 mg sodium, 17 g carbohydrates, 0 g fiber

2

Sprinkle Egg Sugar Cookies

Active Time 25 minutes
Total Time 40 minutes
Makes 36 to 48 (depending on size and shape)

- 1 batch Classic Sugar Cookie Dough (page 18)
- 1 batch Royal Icing (page 24)
  Green, pink, blue and yellow food coloring
  Sprinkles and nonpareils, for decorating

1. Prepare cookies per recipe instructions, using floured egg-shaped cookie cutters to cut out shapes. Let cool completely before decorating.

2. While cookies cool, prepare the Royal Icing through Step 2. Add water 1 teaspoon at a time to make a thick drizzling consistency, then divide among 4 bowls. Tint light green, pink, blue and yellow; transfer to piping bags fitted with small round tips.

3. Outline and fill in cookies with icings. (For icing tips, see page 26.) Let set for 3 minutes, then decorate with sprinkles and nonpareils.

PER SERVING

About 115 calories, 4 g fat (3 g saturated fat), 1 g protein, 30 mg sodium, 18 g carbohydrates, 0 g fiber

Lemon Curd Egg Cookies

The "yolks" in these cookies are bright, tart and zesty. (Hint: It's lemon curd. Go with store-bought or make your own from scratch.)

Active Time 1 hour | **Total Time** 1 hour 30 minutes, plus cooling | **Makes** 18 to 24 (depending on size and shape)

For the Cookies

1 batch Classic Sugar Cookie Dough (page 18)

For the Buttercream

½ cup (1 stick) unsalted butter, at room temperature

2 cups granulated sugar

1 teaspoon pure vanilla extract

Pinch kosher salt

For Assembly

1 11- to 12-ounce jar lemon curd

Confectioners' sugar, for dusting

1. Prepare cookies per recipe instructions, using floured egg-shaped cookie cutters to cut out shapes. Using a smaller round cutter, cut middles out of half the cookies. Let cool completely before decorating.

2. Meanwhile, prepare the buttercream: Using an electric mixer, beat butter and sugar in a large bowl on medium-high speed until stiff peaks form, about 2 minutes. Add vanilla and salt, and mix to combine.

3. Working one at a time, spread 2 teaspoons buttercream onto each cookie without a hole. Top with cutout cookies. Dust with confectioners' sugar, then fill each hole with 1 teaspoon lemon curd.

PER SERVING
About 295 calories, 13 g fat (8 g saturated fat), 2 g protein, 60 mg sodium, 43 g carbohydrates, 0 g fiber

---

Bonus Recipe!
Homemade Lemon Curd

In a heavy 2-quart saucepan, combine **1 cup granulated sugar, 6 tablespoons (¾ stick) unsalted butter, 1 tablespoon lemon zest, ⅔ cup lemon juice, 1 tablespoon cornstarch** and **¼ teaspoon kosher salt**. Bring to a boil on medium; boil 1 minute, then remove from heat. In a small bowl, lightly beat **5 large egg yolks**. Whisk ¼ cup lemon mixture into yolks (this tempers them). Then whisk entire yolk mixture into lemon mixture in saucepan. Return to medium-low and cook, stirring constantly, until thickened, about 5 minutes. Pour lemon curd into a bowl, cover surface area with plastic wrap and refrigerate until chilled, about 3 hours. Store in the refrigerator for up to a week. Makes about 1⅔ cups.

Candy Cottontail Cookies

Frosting, candies and mini marshmallows turn a batch of plain sugar cookies into bunny-butt treats that'll have your kids giggling all through the egg hunt. Even better, this project is so simple that little ones can help — no ifs, ands or ... well, you know.

Active Time 25 minutes | **Total Time** 45 minutes | **Makes** 12

1 batch Classic Sugar Cookie Dough (page 18)

1 batch Vanilla Buttercream (page 25)

Pink gel food coloring

12 mini marshmallows

24 pink M&M's

72 candy-coated sunflower seeds

1. Prepare cookies per recipe instructions, using a floured 3-inch round cookie cutter to cut out shapes for body and a floured 1-inch oval-shaped cutter to cut out shapes for feet. Let cool completely before decorating.

2. Prepare the Vanilla Buttercream. Divide the buttercream between 2 bowls and tint one portion with pink gel food coloring.

3. To decorate, spread white frosting onto cooled oval cookies and pink frosting onto cooled round cookies. Press ovals into edges of rounds, then press mini marshmallows into centers for tails. Place M&M's in middle of feet and sunflower seeds on edges of feet for toes. Let set, about 2 hours.

PER SERVING
About 610 calories, 33 g fat (20 g saturated fat), 4 g protein, 160 mg sodium, 75 g carbohydrates, 1 g fiber

---

Cookie Cheat!
Short on time? Start with **store-bought refrigerated dough**.
Roll out dough, cut rounds and ovals, bake, and then follow the decorating directions above.

Chocolate-Dipped Macaroons

GLUTEN FREE RECIPE

These sweet cookies are crisp on the outside, chewy on the inside and finished with a dip in chocolate. With only a few ingredients, these tasty goodies are a traditional Passover treat.

Active Time 45 minutes | **Total Time** 2 hours 15 minutes | **Makes** 36

1   14-ounce can sweetened condensed milk

1   teaspoon pure almond extract

½   teaspoon kosher salt

¼   cup almond flour

14 ounces sweetened flaked coconut

12 ounces bittersweet chocolate

≷ INGREDIENT ≷
SPOTLIGHT

Sweetened Condensed Milk

Thick, creamy and sticky sweet, this most important ingredient provides instant flavor with little effort.

1. In a large bowl, whisk together condensed milk, almond extract and salt. Whisk in almond flour until well blended. Add coconut and mix well to coat. Refrigerate for 1½ hours, stirring twice.

2. Heat oven to 350°F. Line 2 baking sheets with parchment paper. Drop mixture by packed heaping tablespoonfuls onto the prepared sheets, spacing them 1 inch apart. Bake, rotating the positions of the baking sheets halfway through, until golden brown around edges, 15 to 16 minutes. Transfer cookies to cooling racks to cool completely.

3. Once cookies are cool, melt chocolate per package directions. Dip bottom of each cookie into chocolate, letting excess drip off, then place on a piece of parchment paper. Once all cookies are dipped, drizzle tops with remaining chocolate and let set.

PER SERVING

About 135 calories, 8 g fat (6 g saturated fat), 2 g protein, 70 mg sodium, 17 g carbohydrates, 2 g fiber

Derby Pie Brownies

Popular in the South during the Kentucky Derby, this pie with a pecan chocolate bourbon filling is said to have been invented in 1950 by the Kern family of Prospect, Kentucky. Instead of pie, whip up a batch of inspired brownies and you're off to the races!

Active Time 15 minutes | **Total Time** 1 hour 10 minutes | **Makes** 16

¾ cup (1 ½ sticks) unsalted butter, cut up

1 ½ cups granulated sugar

1 ¼ cups unsweetened cocoa powder

½ teaspoon kosher salt

½ teaspoon pure vanilla extract

3 large eggs

¾ cup all-purpose flour

1 cup pecan halves

3 tablespoons turbinado sugar

1 tablespoon bourbon

1. Position a rack in the lower third of the oven and heat to 325°F. Line an 8-inch square baking pan with parchment paper, leaving a 2-inch overhang on two opposite sides.

2. In a medium saucepan, melt butter on low. Add sugar, cocoa and salt, and cook, stirring, until combined, about 5 minutes.

3. Remove from heat and stir in vanilla. Add eggs, one at a time, stirring until fully incorporated. Fold in flour until combined. Transfer batter to the prepared pan.

4. In a small bowl, toss pecans with turbinado sugar and bourbon. Sprinkle nuts over brownie batter and bake until brownies are set and a toothpick inserted 2 inches from center comes out almost clean, with a few moist crumbs attached, 50 to 55 minutes. Let cool completely in the pan. Use overhangs to transfer to a cutting board and then cut into pieces.

PER SERVING
About 255 calories, 15 g fat (6.5 g saturated fat), 4 g protein, 75 mg sodium, 31 g carbohydrates, 3 g fiber

Jasmine Madeleines with Lemon & Poppy Seed Glaze

Tea is the surprise ingredient in this fragrant, delicate dessert that's perfect for celebratory brunches of all varieties, from Mother's Day to bridal showers.

Active Time 25 minutes | **Total Time** 35 minutes, plus chilling | **Makes** 18

2/3 cup all-purpose flour, plus more for the pan

1 teaspoon baking powder

¼ teaspoon kosher salt

½ cup (1 stick) unsalted butter, plus more melted for the pan

3 tablespoons loose jasmine tea

⅓ cup granulated sugar

2 large eggs, at room temperature

2 tablespoons whole milk

¾ cup confectioners' sugar

1 tablespoon fresh lemon juice

½ teaspoon poppy seeds

Cookie Cheat!

White Chocolate & Lavender Madeleines

Dip **store-bought madeleines** into **melted white chocolate**, sprinkle with **dried lavender** and let set.

1. In a large bowl, whisk together flour, baking powder and salt; set aside. In a medium saucepan, melt butter. Add tea and let steep 5 minutes. Strain through a wire-mesh strainer lined with cheesecloth; discard tea. Set aside.

2. In a bowl, whisk together granulated sugar and eggs until pale and slightly thickened, 2 to 3 minutes. Gently fold in flour mixture, then fold in melted butter until fully incorporated. Stir in milk (batter should be smooth and shiny). Press a piece of plastic wrap against surface of batter; refrigerate until chilled, 1 hour or up to 2 days.

3. When ready to bake, place a rimmed baking sheet in the oven and heat to 400°F. Brush a madeleine pan with melted butter; dust with flour, tapping out excess.

4. Pour 1 tablespoon batter into each mold of the madeleine pan. (There will be some leftover batter for a second batch.) Place the pan on the preheated baking sheet. Bake until golden brown and big bumps on top spring back when touched, 11 to 13 minutes. Remove the pan from the oven and immediately release madeleines by rapping the pan on the counter. Transfer to a cooling rack to cool completely. Repeat with remaining batter.

5. In a bowl, whisk together confectioners' sugar, lemon juice and poppy seeds (thin with water if needed); drizzle over madeleines.

PER SERVING

About 110 calories, 6 g fat (4 g saturated fat), 1 g protein, 65 mg sodium, 13 g carbohydrates, 0 g fiber

Kleicha

Popularly served for Eid al-Fitr, the feast to celebrate the end of Ramadan fasting, these traditional Iraqi cookies can (and should!) be enjoyed year-round.

Active Time 1 hour 5 minutes | **Total Time** 1 hour 55 minutes, plus rising and cooling | **Makes** 22

For the Dough

6 to 9	tablespoons warm water (about 120°F)
1½	teaspoons active dry yeast
2	teaspoons honey
½	cup (1 stick) unsalted butter, melted and warm
2½	cups all-purpose flour, plus more for rolling
¾	teaspoon kosher salt
2	teaspoons nigella seed or 1 teaspoon cumin seed, both optional
1	large egg, beaten well
1½	teaspoons sesame seeds

For the Filling

10	ounces medjool dates, pitted (about 15 large dates)
½	teaspoon cinnamon
¾	teaspoon ground cardamom
2	tablespoons melted extra virgin coconut oil or safflower oil
⅓	cup boiling water
¼	teaspoon kosher salt

1. Using an electric mixer, beat together 6 tablespoons warm water, yeast and honey; let stand until mixture starts to foam, 10 minutes. Add butter and then flour, salt and, if using, nigella or cumin seed. Mix on low speed until flour is just incorporated and dough is hydrated but not sticky, adding up to 3 more tablespoons water as necessary.

2. Transfer dough to work surface and knead lightly to form a mass, then return to the bowl. Cover tightly with plastic wrap and let rise in a warm place, 40 minutes.

3. Heat oven to 350°F, and make the date filling: In a food processor, combine filling ingredients and process until a somewhat smooth paste forms. Date mixture should be spreadable. Adjust with a bit more water if necessary. Divide the dough in half and wrap one half in plastic.

4. Dust a large piece of parchment paper with flour. Place dough on top and form into a square. Sprinkle with flour and roll into a 12-inch square, ⅛ to 1/16 inch thick. (Slide a long offset metal spatula underneath to make sure dough can release from parchment.)

5. Dollop half the date mixture onto dough; spread evenly with an offset spatula, bringing mixture fully to the edge closest to you and within an inch of all other edges.

6. Starting with edge closest to you, roll dough tightly into a log and flip seam side down. Gently press to flatten slightly. Brush surface with beaten egg and then sprinkle half the sesame seeds on top. Using a serrated knife, cut dough on a slight bias into 1-inch-thick rounds.

7. Place slices, seam side down, upright on a parchment-lined baking sheet, spacing them 3 inches apart. Bake, rotating the positions of the baking sheets halfway through, until golden brown, 20 to 22 minutes. Transfer to a cooling rack to let cool. Repeat with remaining dough and filling.

PER SERVING

About 155 calories, 6 g fat (4 g saturated fat), 2 g protein, 95 mg sodium, 24 g carbohydrates, 2 g fiber

Fossil Cookies

Whether it's Earth Day, Halloween, a birthday or any given Wednesday, these cookies make for a fun, kid-friendly activity — and an excuse to talk about science.

Active Time 45 minutes | **Total Time** 1 hour 15 minutes | **Makes** 72 to 96 (depending on size and shape)

For the Cookies

- 1 batch Black Cocoa Cookie Dough (page 21)
- 1 batch Classic Sugar Cookie Dough (page 18)
- Plastic toy insects, to make designs

For the Glaze

- 1 1/3 cups confectioners' sugar
- 4 tablespoons water
- 2 tablespoons heavy cream
- Food coloring

Switch It Up!

These cookies are great for kids' parties and Halloween, but if you select different shapes and colors of glaze, they can work for any holiday or party.

1. Prepare cookie doughs as directed. After rolling and chilling, break into irregular shapes and transfer to parchment-lined baking sheets, spacing them 2 inches apart. Once dough has softened a bit, gently press plastic toy insects into each cookie to make indentations. Refrigerate dough until firm, about 30 minutes.

2. Heat oven to 350°F. Bake, rotating the positions of the baking sheets halfway through, until cookies are just set around edges, 10 to 12 minutes. Let cool on baking sheets for 5 minutes before transferring to cooling racks to cool completely.

3. Meanwhile, make the glaze: In a large bowl, whisk together sugar, water and heavy cream until sugar is dissolved and no lumps remain. Adjust with additional water if needed and color with food coloring if desired.

4. Place cookies on a cooling rack set over parchment paper and spoon glaze on top. Use a spoon to push glaze off sides of cookies so you can see the fossil indentations.

PER SERVING

About 85 calories, 4 g fat (3 g saturated fat), 1 g protein, 35 mg sodium, 11 g carbohydrates, 0 g fiber

Mixed Berry & Ice Cream Whoopie Pies

Bring a bit of patriotic flair to backyard BBQ parties with these festive cookie sandwiches.

Active Time 20 minutes | **Total Time** 50 minutes, plus chilling | **Makes** 16

2 ¼   cups all-purpose flour

¾   teaspoon baking powder

½   teaspoon kosher salt

¼   teaspoon baking soda

½   cup (1 stick) unsalted butter, at room temperature

½   cup granulated sugar

½   cup packed light brown sugar

1   tablespoon grated lemon zest

1   large egg

1   cup buttermilk

6   ounces small blueberries and raspberries

1   pint ice cream

1. Heat oven to 375°F. Line 3 large baking sheets with parchment paper. In a medium bowl, whisk together flour, baking powder, salt and baking soda; set aside.

2. Using an electric mixer, beat butter, sugars and lemon zest in a large bowl on medium-high speed until light and fluffy, about 3 minutes. Reduce speed to low and beat in egg. In two additions, alternately add flour mixture and buttermilk, mixing until just incorporated. Gently fold in berries.

3. Scoop 32 mounds of batter (about 1½ tablespoons each) onto the prepared sheets, spacing them 2 inches apart. Bake in batches until puffed and the tops spring back when lightly pressed, 12 to 14 minutes. Let cool on baking sheets for 5 minutes before transferring to a cooling rack to cool completely.

4. Form sandwiches with cooled cookies and 2 tablespoons ice cream for each sandwich.

PER SERVING
About 220 calories, 8 g fat (5 g saturated fat), 3 g protein, 140 mg sodium, 32 g carbohydrates, 0 g fiber

Blueberry Whoopie Pies

For a summery take on the classic whoopie pie, take advantage of peak-season berries found at pick-your-own farms, roadside produce stands or your local grocery store. Pair the berry-studded cookies with a velvety lemon-mascarpone filling.

Active Time 30 minutes | **Total Time** 1 hour 10 minutes, plus cooling | **Makes** 16

For the Cookies

2 ¼	cups all-purpose flour
¾	teaspoon baking powder
½	teaspoon kosher salt
¼	teaspoon baking soda
½	cup (1 stick) unsalted butter, at room temperature
½	cup granulated sugar
½	cup packed light brown sugar
1	tablespoon lemon zest
1	large egg
1	cup buttermilk
6	ounces blueberries

For the Filling

1	8-ounce container mascarpone cheese
1	tablespoon lemon zest
¼	cup confectioners' sugar
3 ½	tablespoons buttermilk
	Pinch kosher salt

1. Prepare the cookies: Heat oven to 375°F. Line 3 large baking sheets with parchment paper. In a medium bowl, whisk together flour, baking powder, salt and baking soda; set aside.

2. Using an electric mixer, beat butter, sugars and lemon zest in a large bowl on medium speed until light and fluffy, 2 to 3 minutes. Beat in egg. Alternately add flour mixture and buttermilk, beginning and ending with flour mixture, until just incorporated. Fold in berries.

3. Scoop cookies (1½ tablespoons each) onto the prepared sheets, spacing them 2 inches apart. Bake, in batches, until puffed and tops spring back when lightly pressed, 12 to 14 minutes. Let cool on baking sheets for 5 minutes before transferring to a cooling rack to cool completely.

4. Meanwhile, make the filling: Using an electric mixer, beat mascarpone, lemon zest, confectioners' sugar, buttermilk and salt in a large bowl on medium speed until blended, about 1 minute.

5. Assemble sandwiches: Spread filling onto bottom of half the cookies, dividing evenly, then top with remaining cookies. Store cookies in an airtight container for up to 2 days.

PER SERVING

About 245 calories, 12 g fat (8 g saturated fat), 4 g protein, 140 mg sodium, 31 g carbohydrates, 1 g fiber

Black-As-Night Cocoa Cookies

What makes these cookies so dark? It's black cocoa powder! Add it to dough, then work some magic to create creepy animals and spooky skeletons for Halloween.

1

Bat Sandwich Cookies

Active Time 25 minutes
Total Time 45 minutes
Makes 25 (depending on size and shape)

- 1 batch Black Cocoa Cookie Dough (page 21)
- 1 batch Royal Icing (page 24)
- 1 batch Vanilla Buttercream (page 25)
  Black gel food coloring
  Black sanding sugar

1. Prepare cookies per recipe instructions, using cocoa-coated bat-shaped cookie cutters to cut out cookies. Bake as directed and let cool completely.

2. While cookies cool, prepare the Royal Icing and Vanilla Buttercream. Tint the Royal Icing with gel food coloring and use to decorate half the cookies. Sprinkle black sanding sugar on top of wet icing and let set. Sandwich pairs of cookies together with Vanilla Buttercream.

   PER SERVING
   About 335 calories, 14 g fat (8 g saturated fat), 2 g protein, 90 mg sodium, 52 g carbohydrates, 1 g fiber

2

Black Cat Cookies

Active Time 25 minutes
Total Time 1 hour
Makes 25 (depending on size and shape)

- 1 batch Black Cocoa Cookie Dough (page 21)
- 1 batch Classic Sugar Cookie Dough (page 18)
- 1 batch Royal Icing (page 24)
  Vodka
  Silver and black luster dust

1. Prepare cookies per recipe instructions, using cocoa-coated cat-shaped cookie cutters to cut out cookies from Black Cocoa Cookie Dough. Use flour-coated round cutters to cut out cookies from Classic Sugar Cookie Dough. Bake as directed and let cool completely.

2. While cookies cool, prepare the Royal Icing. Use the icing to outline and fill in cooled sugar cookies and attach cat cookies on top. In a small bowl, mix a touch of vodka with silver luster dust and then use a small brush to paint streaks onto white icing. Repeat with black luster dust and use it to paint small bat silhouettes onto the icing. Let set.

   PER SERVING
   About 330 calories, 14 g fat (8 g saturated fat), 4 g protein, 120 mg sodium, 49 g carbohydrates, 1 g fiber

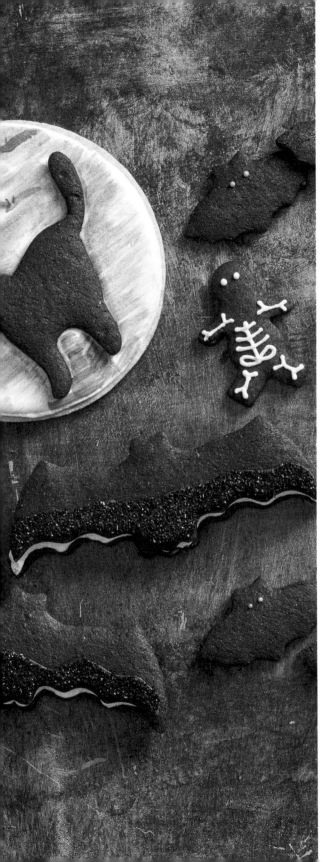

3

Baby Bat & Skeleton Cookies

Active Time 25 minutes
Total Time 40 minutes
Makes 50 (depending on size and shape)

1 batch Black Cocoa Cookie Dough (page 21)
1 batch Royal Icing (page 24)
Gel food coloring, optional

1. Prepare cookies per recipe instructions, using cocoa-coated small bat-shaped and gingerbread man cutters to cut out bats and skeletons from dough. Bake as directed and let cool completely.

2. While cookies cool, prepare the Royal Icing and tint if desired. Transfer icing to a piping bag fitted with a small round tip. Pipe bones onto each skeleton and eyes onto each bat. Let set.

PER SERVING
About 95 calories, 3 g fat (2 g saturated fat), 1 g protein, 35 mg sodium, 16 g carbohydrates, 0 g fiber

≈ INGREDIENT ≈
SPOTLIGHT

Black Cocoa

Dutch process cocoa is treated with an alkalizing agent to reduce its acidity for a deeper flavor. Black cocoa is more heavily Dutched and has the most intense chocolate taste.

Moss Cookies

Spread misshapen cookies with green frosting and top with cookie and graham cracker crumbs to create an enchanted forest-floor scene, perfect for any Halloween party.

Active Time 25 minutes | **Total Time** 40 minutes | **Makes** 36

2 ¾   cups all-purpose flour

½   teaspoon baking powder

½   teaspoon kosher salt

1   cup (2 sticks) unsalted butter, at room temperature

¾   cup granulated sugar
    Green gel food coloring

1   large egg

1   teaspoon pure vanilla extract

½   cup Vanilla Buttercream (page 25)

2   graham crackers

≈ TEST
≈ KITCHEN ≈
TIP

These mossy crumbs are great for adding spooky details to cakes, pudding cups or cupcakes. They can also be the backdrop for a Halloween cookie plate; just top with coffins (page 220) or bats and cats (page 216).

1. Heat oven to 350°F. Line 2 large baking sheets with parchment paper. In a large bowl, whisk together flour, baking powder and salt; set aside.

2. Using an electric mixer, beat butter and sugar in a large bowl on medium-high speed until light and fluffy, about 3 minutes. During the last minute, add a few dabs of gel food coloring to make a dark green color. Beat in egg and then vanilla.

3. Reduce speed to low and gradually add flour mixture, mixing until just incorporated.

4. Using an offset spatula or the palm of your hand, take unevenly sized pieces of dough and spread into thin, rough cookie shapes (about ⅛ to ¼ inch thick). Place dough onto the prepared sheets, spacing them 2 inches apart.

5. Bake, rotating the positions of the baking sheets halfway through, until cookies feel sandy on top, 13 to 15 minutes. Let cool on a cooling rack.

6. Prepare the Vanilla Buttercream as directed. To decorate, tint buttercream green. Finely crumble graham crackers and 2 moss cookies. Working one at a time, lightly spread underside of remaining cookies with a thin layer of frosting and immediately sprinkle with cookie crumbs.

PER SERVING

About 120 calories, 6 g fat (4 g saturated fat), 1 g protein, 45 mg sodium, 14 g carbohydrates, 0 g fiber

Coffin Sandwich Cookies

Bakers, beware! These haunted sweets hide a secret inside. All right, it's a rich and creamy buttercream filling, but you've been warned.

Active Time 2 hours 20 minutes | **Total Time** 3 hours 45 minutes | **Makes** 34

For the Cookies

- ⅓ cup cornstarch
- 2 tablespoons unsweetened cocoa powder
- ¾ teaspoon kosher salt
- 1 cup (2 sticks) unsalted butter, at room temperature
- 1 cup packed light brown sugar
- ½ cup molasses
- 2 large eggs
- 5 cups all-purpose flour

For the White Chocolate Bones

- ½ cup white chocolate candy melts

For the Filling

- ½ cup (1 stick) unsalted butter, at room temperature
- 1½ cups sifted confectioners' sugar
- ¼ teaspoon pure vanilla extract
- Pinch kosher salt
- Red food coloring
- Orange food coloring

For the Icing

- 1 batch Decorator's Icing (page 25)
- Black food coloring

1. Make the cookies: In a large bowl, whisk together cornstarch, cocoa and salt; set aside.

2. Using an electric mixer, beat butter and sugar in a large bowl on medium speed until light and fluffy, about 3 minutes. Add molasses and mix until incorporated, 1 minute. Beat in eggs, one at a time, scraping the bottom and the side of the bowl after each addition.

3. Reduce speed to medium-low and mix in cornstarch mixture, then flour, mixing until just incorporated. Shape dough into 2 disks and roll each between 2 sheets of parchment paper to ⅛ to ¼ inch thick. Chill until firm, 30 minutes in the refrigerator or 15 minutes in the freezer.

4. Heat oven to 375°F. Line 4 baking sheets with parchment paper. Using a floured coffin-shaped cutter, cut out cookies and place them onto the prepared sheets, spacing them 2 inches apart. Reroll, chill and cut scraps.

5. Bake, rotating the positions of the baking sheets halfway through, until cookies are set around edges but still a little soft in the center, 8 to 9 minutes. Let cool on baking sheets for 5 minutes before transferring to cooling racks to cool completely.

6. Make the white chocolate bones: Melt candy melts according to package directions. Transfer to a resealable plastic bag and snip a small hole in one corner. Fill a bone-shaped chocolate mold with melted candy or pipe bone shapes onto a parchment-lined baking sheet. Refrigerate until firm, 20 to 30 minutes. Tap out of molds.

7. Make the filling: Using an electric mixer, beat butter in a large bowl on medium speed until smooth and creamy, 1 to 2 minutes. Add confectioners' sugar, ½ cup at a time, mixing until incorporated. Mix in vanilla and salt. Use red and orange food coloring to dye a deep orange color.

8. Make the Decorator's Icing. Transfer half the icing to a small bowl and cover with a piece of plastic wrap, pressing directly onto the surface; set aside. Using black food coloring, tint remaining icing gray. Transfer to a resealable plastic bag and snip a very small hole in one corner (or use a piping bag fitted with a fine round tip). Use a pastry brush to lightly brush white icing onto tops of half the cookies. Run a fork through icing to make a wood grain; let set. Pipe gray icing borders and decorations onto iced cookies; let set.

9. Frost or pipe orange filling onto plain cookies and sandwich together with decorated tops. Decorate edges with white chocolate bones.

PER SERVING
About 70 calories, 3 g fat (2 g saturated fat), 1 g protein, 50 mg sodium, 9 g carbohydrates, 0 g fiber

Nankhatai

Made with ghee, cardamom, nutmeg and two types of flour (whole-wheat and semolina), these Indian shortbread cookies are nutty, buttery and excellent when eaten slighty warm.

Active Time 45 minutes | **Total Time** 1 hour 30 minutes | **Makes** 16

1 ½ cups whole-wheat flour, preferably stone ground

⅓ cup semolina

1 teaspoon kosher salt

⅔ cup ghee, at room temperature, preferably homemade

¾ cup confectioners' sugar

½ teaspoon ground cardamom

½ teaspoon freshly grated nutmeg

1 heaping tablespoon shelled pistachios, roughly chopped

Bonus Recipe!

Homemade Ghee

Cut **1½ pounds unsalted butter** into small pieces, place in a medium heavy-bottomed saucepan and melt over medium-low. Once melted, reduce heat to lowest setting and simmer, undisturbed, until milk solids separate and fall to the bottom of the pot and the liquid becomes a clear golden color, 15 to 20 minutes. Tilt the pot slightly to skim off and discard any foam. Continue to cook, without stirring, until the solids on the bottom begin to caramelize and there is a nutty aroma, about 15 minutes more. Turn off heat and let cool for 5 minutes. Line a strainer with 4 layers of cheesecloth and set over a large jar. Strain butter, leaving browned solids in the pot. Let cool to room temperature, cover tightly and refrigerate until ready to use.

1. In a small bowl, whisk together flour, semolina and salt; set aside.

2. Using an electric mixer, beat ghee, confectioners' sugar, cardamom and nutmeg in a large bowl on medium-high speed until lightened in color, 2 to 3 minutes. Reduce speed to low and mix in flour mixture until just combined (dough may be slightly clumpy, similar to pie dough). Transfer dough to a piece of plastic wrap and form into a 1-inch-thick disk. Wrap well and refrigerate until slightly firm, 15 minutes.

3. Heat oven to 350°F. Line 2 baking sheets with parchment paper. Roll dough into balls slightly less than 1½ inches in diameter (about 1 ounce each) and place onto the prepared sheets, spacing them 3 inches apart. Flatten each ball to ¾ inch thick (crackly edges are totally fine). If desired, using a sharp knife, make a cross indentation about ⅛ inch deep into each cookie. Press a few pieces of chopped pistachio into center of cookies.

4. Bake, rotating the positions of the baking sheets halfway through, until set and golden brown on bottoms, 14 to 18 minutes (Cookies will be more tender at 14 minutes. If you like a crunchier cookie, bake to the longer end of the range.) Transfer cookies to a cooling rack and let cool completely.

PER SERVING
About 150 calories, 9 g fat (5 g saturated fat), 2 g protein, 120 mg sodium, 16 g carbohydrates, 1 g fiber

TEST
KITCHEN
TIP

For a more tender,
crumbly cookie,
replace ½ cup of the
whole-wheat flour with
chickpea flour.

Chocolate Chip Mandel Bread

Similar to biscotti, these classic Jewish cookies (also known as mandelbrot) are twice baked, making them crunchy, long-lasting and perfect for dipping into coffee or tea.

Active Time 25 minutes | **Total Time** 1 hour 40 minutes | **Makes** 40

3 ¼ cups all-purpose flour

1 teaspoon baking powder

½ teaspoon kosher salt

1 ½ teaspoons ground cinnamon

3 large eggs

1 cup canola oil

1 teaspoon pure vanilla extract

1 ¼ cups granulated sugar

1 cup semisweet chocolate chips

1 cup walnuts, roughly chopped

1. Heat oven to 375°F. Line 2 baking sheets with parchment paper. In a medium bowl, whisk together flour, baking powder, salt and ½ teaspoon cinnamon; set aside.

2. Using an electric mixer, beat eggs in a large bowl on medium speed until foamy, about 3 minutes. Mix in oil, vanilla and ¾ cup sugar. Reduce speed to medium-low and gradually mix in flour mixture until fully incorporated. Fold in chocolate chips and walnuts.

3. In a shallow dish, combine remaining ½ cup sugar and 1 teaspoon cinnamon. Divide dough into 6 equal portions and shape each into a 2-inch-wide loaf. Roll in cinnamon-sugar mixture and transfer to the prepared sheets, spacing them 1 inch apart.

4. Bake until loaves are set and golden brown, 15 to 20 minutes. Let cool on baking sheets for 10 minutes before transferring to a cooling rack to cool for 20 minutes more. Reduce oven temperature to 350°F.

5. Slice loaves on a slight diagonal into ¾-inch-thick pieces. Place cut side up on the baking sheets, spacing them ½ inch apart. Bake until light golden brown, 12 to 15 minutes. Let cool at least 5 minutes before serving.

PER SERVING

About 155 calories, 9 g fat (9 g saturated fat), 2 g protein, 45 mg sodium, 17 g carbohydrates, 1 g fiber

Chai Tree & Snowflake Cookies

Thanks to nutmeg, cardamom, cloves, ginger, cinnamon and black pepper, these cookies are the definition of sugar and spice and everything nice.

Active Time 25 minutes | **Total Time** 40 minutes, plus chilling and cooling | **Makes** 50

2 ¾   cups all-purpose flour

½   teaspoon baking powder

¼   teaspoon kosher salt

1 ½   teaspoons ground ginger

1   teaspoon ground cinnamon

½   teaspoon ground cloves

½   teaspoon nutmeg

½   teaspoon cardamom

⅛   teaspoon black pepper

1   cup (2 sticks) unsalted butter, at room temperature

¾   cup granulated sugar

1   large egg

1 ½   teaspoons pure vanilla extract

    Royal Icing (page 24), for decorating

1. In a large bowl, whisk together flour, baking powder, salt, ground ginger, cinnamon, cloves, nutmeg, cardamom and black pepper; set aside.

2. Using an electric mixer, beat butter and sugar in another large bowl on medium speed until light and fluffy, about 3 minutes. Beat in egg and then vanilla.

3. Reduce speed to low and gradually add flour mixture, mixing until just incorporated. Shape dough into 2 disks and roll each between 2 sheets of parchment paper to ⅛ inch thick. Chill until firm, 30 minutes in the refrigerator or 15 minutes in the freezer.

4. Heat oven to 350°F. Line 2 baking sheets with parchment paper. Using floured cookie cutters, cut out cookies. Place onto the prepared sheets, spacing them 2 inches apart. Reroll, chill and cut scraps.

5. Bake, rotating the positions of the baking sheets halfway through, until light golden brown around edges, 10 to 12 minutes. Let cool on baking sheets for 5 minutes before transferring to cooling racks to cool completely.

6. While cookies cool, prepare the Royal Icing. Decorate cooled cookies with icing.

PER SERVING
About 90 calories, 4 g fat (2 g saturated fat), 1 g protein, 20 mg sodium, 13 g carbohydrates, 0 g fiber

Fruitcake Crisps

Inspired by British fruitcakes, which are incredibly popular during the holidays, these cookies are studded with candied and dried fruit as well as nuts.

Active Time 25 minutes | **Total Time** 40 minutes, plus chilling and cooling | **Makes** 50

2 ¾	cups all-purpose flour
½	teaspoon baking powder
¼	teaspoon kosher salt
1	cup (2 sticks) unsalted butter, at room temperature
¾	cup granulated sugar
1	large egg
1 ½	teaspoons pure vanilla extract
⅓	cup chopped candied citrus (orange and lemon)
⅓	cup chopped pistachios
½	cup dried cranberries

1. In a large bowl, whisk together flour, baking powder and salt; set aside.

2. Using an electric mixer, beat butter and sugar in another large bowl on medium speed until light and fluffy, about 3 minutes. Beat in egg and then vanilla.

3. Reduce speed to low and gradually add flour mixture, mixing until just incorporated. Fold in candied citrus, pistachios and dried cranberries. Shape dough into 2 logs, each 2 inches thick. Wrap and flatten slightly to create an oval; freeze for 20 minutes.

4. Heat oven to 350°F. Line 2 baking sheets with parchment paper. Cut logs into ½-inch-thick slices and place onto the prepared sheets, spacing them 2 inches apart.

5. Bake, rotating the positions of the baking sheets halfway through, until light golden brown around edges, 12 to 14 minutes. Let cool on baking sheets for 5 minutes before transferring to cooling racks to cool completely.

PER SERVING

About 85 calories, 4 g fat (2 g saturated fat), 1 g protein, 20 mg sodium, 11 g carbohydrates, 0 g fiber

Gingerbread Man S'mores

Although the gingerbread is irresistible — with a combo of ginger, cinnamon, nutmeg, cloves and molasses — what kicks this cookie into overdrive is a layer of bittersweet chocolate and marshmallow–cream cheese frosting.

Active Time 1 hour 10 minutes | **Total Time** 2 hours 45 minutes | **Makes** 23

2 1/2	cups all-purpose flour
2 1/2	teaspoons ground ginger
1 1/2	teaspoons ground cinnamon
1/2	teaspoon ground nutmeg
1/2	teaspoon baking soda
1/4	teaspoon ground cloves
1/4	teaspoon kosher salt
1/2	cup (1 stick) unsalted butter, at room temperature
1/2	cup firmly packed dark brown sugar
1	large egg
1/4	cup molasses
1 1/2	teaspoons pure vanilla extract
1	cup bittersweet chocolate chips
1	8-ounce package cream cheese
1	cup marshmallow cream
	Large red nonpareils or red mini candies, for decorating

1. In a large bowl, whisk together flour, ginger, cinnamon, nutmeg, baking soda, cloves and salt; set aside.

2. Using an electric mixer, beat butter and sugar in another large bowl until light and fluffy, about 3 minutes. Beat in egg, molasses and vanilla. Reduce speed to low and gradually add flour mixture, mixing until just incorporated (dough will be soft).

3. Shape dough into 4 disks, making each 1 inch thick, and then roll each disk between 2 sheets of parchment paper to 1/8 inch thick. Refrigerate until firm, about 30 minutes.

4. Heat oven to 350°F. Line 2 baking sheets with parchment paper. Using floured 3 1/2-inch gingerbread man cutters, cut out cookies from dough. Place onto the prepared sheets, spacing them 1 inch apart. Reroll, chill and cut scraps.

5. Bake, rotating the positions of the baking sheets halfway through, until cookies start to turn golden brown around edges, 10 to 12 minutes. Let cool on baking sheets for 3 minutes before transferring to a cooling rack to cool completely.

6. Meanwhile, melt chocolate chips in the microwave according to package directions. Spread 1 teaspoon melted chocolate onto flat side of half the cookies. Place cookies, chocolate side up, onto the baking sheet and refrigerate until just set, about 10 minutes.

7. Using an electric mixer, beat cream cheese and marshmallow cream in a large bowl until fluffy, about 2 minutes. Spread 1 rounded teaspoon marshmallow filling onto flat side of remaining cookies. Sandwich with chocolate-sided cookies and refrigerate until set, about 20 minutes.

8. Transfer remaining marshmallow filling to a piping bag fitted with a writing tip (or a resealable plastic bag; snip off a corner). Decorate as desired with filling and red nonpareils.

PER SERVING
About 225 calories, 11 g fat (7 g saturated fat), 3 g protein, 90 mg sodium, 27 g carbohydrates, 1 g fiber

Gingerbread Sandwich Cookies

Double up on the gingerbread goodness by stacking two cookies and layering a rich milk chocolate frosting in between.

Active Time 30 minutes | **Total Time** 1 hour | **Makes** 24

For the Cookies

2 1/2	cups all-purpose flour
2 1/2	teaspoons ground ginger
1 1/2	teaspoons ground cinnamon
1/2	teaspoon freshly grated nutmeg
1/2	teaspoon baking soda
1/4	teaspoon ground cloves
1/4	teaspoon kosher salt
1/2	cup (1 stick) unsalted butter, at room temperature
1/2	cup firmly packed dark brown sugar
1	large egg
1/4	cup molasses
1 1/2	teaspoons pure vanilla extract
	Royal Icing (page 24)
	Sanding sugar and white pearl dragées, for decorating

For the Frosting

1/2	cup (1 stick) unsalted butter, at room temperature
1/3	cup confectioners' sugar
	Kosher salt
4	ounces milk chocolate, melted and cooled to room temperature

1. Make the cookies: In a large bowl, whisk together flour, ginger, cinnamon, nutmeg, baking soda, cloves and salt; set aside.

2. Using an electric mixer, beat butter and brown sugar in another large bowl on high speed until light and fluffy, 4 to 6 minutes. Beat in egg, molasses and vanilla. Reduce speed to low and gradually add flour mixture, mixing until just incorporated (dough will be soft).

3. Shape dough into 3 disks and roll each between 2 sheets of parchment paper to 1/8 inch thick. Chill until firm, 30 minutes in the refrigerator or 15 minutes in the freezer.

4. Heat oven to 350°F. Line 2 baking sheets with parchment paper. Using floured cookie cutters, cut out cookies. Place onto the prepared sheets, spacing them 2 inches apart.

5. Bake, rotating the positions of the baking sheets halfway through, until light golden brown around edges, 10 to 12 minutes. Let cool on baking sheets for 5 minutes before transferring to a cooling rack to cool completely.

6. Meanwhile, make chocolate frosting: Using an electric mixer, beat butter, sugar and a pinch of salt in a large bowl on medium speed until light and fluffy, 2 minutes. Reduce speed to low and add melted chocolate, beating to combine.

7. Prepare the Royal Icing. Decorate half the cookies with icing, sanding sugar and dragées as desired. Spread chocolate frosting onto remaining cookie halves and sandwich with decorated halves.

PER SERVING

About 226 calories, 9 g fat (6 g saturated fat), 2 g protein, 65 mg sodium, 34 g carbohydrates, 1 g fiber

Reindeer & Tree Cookies

Here's proof that intricately iced cookies can taste as good as they look. Add dimension to reindeer noses and trees with silver and gold sugar pearls, or boost the cookies' shimmer by piping gold Royal Icing onto the reindeer antlers. (See photo, page 186.)

Active Time 25 minutes
Total Time 40 minutes, plus chilling and cooling
Makes 50 (depending on size and shape)

1   batch Classic Sugar Cookie Dough (page 18)

Red, green, white and gold Royal Icing (page 24)

Sanding sugars and sugar pearls, for decorating

Prepare cookies per recipe instructions, cutting into reindeer and tree shapes with cookie cutters. Let cool completely before decorating as desired.

PER SERVING
About 275 calories, 13 g fat (7 g saturated fat), 4 g protein, 265 mg sodium, 38 g carbohydrates, 1 g fiber

Polar Bear Sugar Cookies

These adorable cookies will fit right in at your ugly sweater party! Even better? Bake up a batch, set out icing and sprinkles, and let guests compete to see who can come up with the ugliest sweater design. Everyone's a winner, though, when they eat their cookie at the end.

Active Time 25 minutes
Total Time 40 minutes, plus chilling and cooling
Makes 50 (depending on size and shape)

1   batch Classic Sugar Cookie Dough (page 18)

Royal Icing (page 24)

Mini brown M&Ms, for decorating

1. Prepare cookies per recipe instructions, using a floured bear-shaped cookie cutter to cut out bears from dough. Let cool completely before decorating.

2. While cookies cool, prepare the Royal Icing. Outline and fill each cooled cookie with white icing, leaving the polar bear's sweater area unfilled. To make a polar bear nose, pipe a mound of stiff icing onto the lower half of the face and let set until almost dry, then press on a mini brown M&M. Pipe on faces, then decorate sweaters, scarves and hats as desired using tinted icing.

PER SERVING
About 110 calories, 4 g fat (2 g saturated fat), 1 g protein, 30 mg sodium, 18 g carbohydrates, 0 g fiber

Holiday Spritz Cookies

Buttery spritz cookies only look bakery-bought! A cookie press makes creating intricate shapes a snap.

Active Time 1 hour | **Total Time** 1 hour 15 minutes, plus decorating | **Makes** 40

1 ¼   cups all-purpose flour

¼   teaspoon kosher salt

½   cup (1 stick) unsalted butter, at room temperature

¼   cup granulated sugar

1   large egg yolk, at room temperature

½   teaspoon pure vanilla extract

Red and green gel food coloring, if desired

Royal Icing (page 24)

Sprinkles, for decorating

≡ **TOOL SPOTLIGHT** ≡

Cookie Press

There's no need to chill or roll out dough thanks to this tool that creates a variety of charming shapes. Just fill with dough, choose a disk and start pressing.

1. Heat oven to 350°F. In a medium bowl, whisk together flour and salt; set aside.

2. Using an electric mixer, beat butter and sugar in a large bowl on high speed until light and fluffy, 4 to 6 minutes. Reduce speed to medium, add egg yolk and vanilla, and beat for 5 minutes.

3. Reduce speed to low and gradually add flour mixture, mixing until just incorporated. Then, using a spatula, fold dough until it forms a ball. If desired, use food coloring to tint some or all of dough.

4. Fill a cookie press with dough according to the manufacturer's instructions. Hold the cookie press so it touches the baking sheet (do not line or grease the baking sheet), then squeeze and lift away, spacing cookies 1 inch apart. (You will need at least 2 large baking sheets.)

5. Bake, rotating the positions of the baking sheets halfway through, until light golden brown around edges, 11 to 13 minutes. Let cool on baking sheets for 1 minute before transferring to a cooling rack to cool completely.

6. While cookies cool, prepare the Royal Icing. Decorate cooled cookies with icing and sprinkles as desired.

PER SERVING
About 60 calories, 3 g fat (2 g saturated fat), 1 g protein, 15 mg sodium, 8 g carbohydrates, 0 g fiber

Chocolate-Almond Spritz Cookies

No cookie press? No problem! These cookies have the flavor of a classic cream cheese spritz, but without the need for the equipment. Just fit a piping bag with a star tip.

Active Time 25 minutes | **Total Time** 1 hour, plus cooling | **Makes** 72

1	cup (2 sticks) unsalted butter, at room temperature
1	8-ounce package cream cheese, at room temperature
1	cup granulated sugar
½	teaspoon kosher salt
1	large egg yolk
1½	teaspoons pure vanilla extract
2½	cups all-purpose flour
5	ounces melted bittersweet chocolate
½	cup finely chopped almond slivers

1. Heat oven to 375°F. Using an electric mixer, beat butter, cream cheese, sugar and salt in a large bowl on medium-high speed until creamy, 3 minutes. Beat in egg yolk and vanilla. Reduce speed to low and add flour, mixing until just incorporated.

2. Transfer dough to a large piping bag fitted with a large open star tip. Pipe dough into 2-inch logs onto baking sheets, spacing them 2 inches apart.

3. Bake until deep golden brown around edges, 12 to 18 minutes. Let cool on baking sheets for 10 minutes before transferring to cooling racks to cool completely.

4. When cool, brush one end of each cookie with melted chocolate, then coat in almonds. Transfer to a piece of parchment paper and let set.

PER SERVING

About 75 calories, 5 g fat (3 g saturated fat), 1 g protein, 25 mg sodium, 7 g carbohydrates, 0 g fiber

Creamy Christmas Light Cookies

Stringing lights just got a whole lot more delicious! Thanks to an assortment of crushed starlight mints, rock candy, dragées, M&M's and string licorice, these bulbs taste great!

Active Time 1 hour 30 minutes | **Total Time** 2 hours 30 minutes | **Makes** 56

3 cups all-purpose flour, plus more for the surface

½ teaspoon kosher salt

1 cup (2 sticks) unsalted butter, at room temperature

2 ounces cream cheese, at room temperature

1 cup granulated sugar

1 large egg

1 teaspoon pure almond extract

½ teaspoon pure vanilla extract

½ batch Vanilla Buttercream (page 25)

Candy for decorating: blue, white and green candy balls; crushed blue starlight mints; silver and white dragées; mint M&M's; white sanding sugar; crushed green and blue rock candy; white nonpareils; shoestring licorice

≡ TEST KITCHEN TIP ≡

Switch up the candies used to adorn each bulb, paying extra attention to the textures of each. If you use a variety of textures, your bulbs will really pop!

1. In a large bowl, whisk together flour and salt; set aside.

2. Using an electric mixer, beat butter, cream cheese and sugar in another large bowl on medium speed until light and fluffy, 2 to 3 minutes. Beat in egg and extracts. Gradually beat in flour mixture until just incorporated. Divide dough in half, flatten into disks and wrap in plastic wrap. Chill for at least 1 hour.

3. Heat oven to 325°F. Line 2 baking sheets with parchment paper. On a floured surface, roll one disk to ¼ inch thickness. Using a 3-inch lightbulb-shaped cookie cutter, cut cookies from dough. Use a skewer to make a hole at the top of each cookie.

4. Bake until golden brown around edges, 11 to 12 minutes. Let cool on baking sheets for 5 minutes before transferring to a cooling rack to cool completely. Repeat with remaining dough, rerolling and cutting scraps only once.

5. While cookies cool, prepare the Vanilla Buttercream. Spread a thin layer of frosting onto each cooled cookie. Decorate with candy as desired. Thread licorice through holes for the wire if desired.

PER SERVING

About 115 calories, 6 g fat (3 g saturated fat), 1 g protein, 30 mg sodium, 16 g carbohydrates, 0 g fiber

GIFT IT!

Place cookies in a glassine-topped box for a fun take on ornament packaging. Add a note that reads "Hope your season is merry and bright."

Chocolate Mittens

Flavor meets fashion with chocolate cutouts shaped like mittens and decorated with beautiful patterns. Too pretty to eat? String them with ribbon and use them as ornaments.

Active Time 2 hours 40 minutes | **Total Time** 3 hours 50 minutes | **Makes** 32

1 batch Black Cocoa Cookie Dough (page 21)

1 batch Royal Icing (page 24)

Red, green, cornflower blue and teal gel food coloring

White, green and blue sanding sugar

1. Prepare cookies per recipe instructions, cutting into mitten shapes using a floured cookie cutter. If using as ornaments, use a straw to poke a small hole on one side of each cuff before baking. Let cool completely before decorating.

2. While cookies cool, prepare the Royal Icing. Divide icing among 4 bowls; tint 3 bowls with gel food coloring as desired. Add water, 1 teaspoon at a time, to thin all icing to the consistency of marshmallow cream. Transfer ⅓ cup of each color icing to piping bags fitted with writing tips. Slightly thin remaining icing in each bowl with 1 teaspoon water. Place thinned icing in separate resealable plastic bags and snip off corners. (You should now have 4 piping bags with thick icing and 4 resealable bags with thinner icing.)

3. To decorate, start with the cuffs. Working with one mitten at a time, use thicker icing to pipe the cuff outline. Squirt some thinner icing of the same color inside the outline; use a brush

Double-Chocolate Peppermint Cookies

Cocoa cookies are filled with a rich chocolate ganache and topped with crushed candy canes for a chocolatey, minty bite-size treat.

Active Time 40 minutes | **Total Time** 1 hour 10 minutes, plus cooling | **Makes** 72

1½   cups all-purpose flour

¼   cup unsweetened cocoa

1   teaspoon baking powder

¼   teaspoon kosher salt

1   12-ounce package bittersweet chocolate chips

½   cup (1 stick) unsalted butter, at room temperature

¾   cup granulated sugar

2   large eggs

6   tablespoons heavy cream

8   candy canes, smashed (about ¾ cup)

1. Heat oven to 350°F. Line 2 baking sheets with parchment paper. In a medium bowl, whisk together flour, cocoa, baking powder and salt; set aside.

2. In a small bowl, melt ½ cup chocolate chips in the microwave in 30-second intervals, stirring between each until melted and smooth. Using an electric mixer, beat butter and sugar in a large bowl on medium-high speed until light and fluffy, about 3 minutes. Beat in eggs, one at a time. Reduce speed to low and gradually add melted chocolate and then flour mixture, mixing until just incorporated. Fold in ¾ cup of remaining chocolate chips.

3. Drop rounded teaspoonfuls of dough onto the prepared sheets, spacing them 2 inches apart. Bake, rotating the positions of the baking sheets halfway through, until cookies are puffed and set, 8 to 10 minutes. Let cool on baking sheets for 2 minutes before transferring to a cooling rack to cool completely.

4. In a medium bowl, microwave heavy cream until simmering, about 30 seconds. Add remaining ¾ cup chocolate chips to cream and let sit for 1 minute. Stir until chocolate is melted and mixture is smooth. Spread about ½ teaspoon chocolate mixture on top of each cookie; top with candy canes. Refrigerate until set, about 20 minutes.

PER SERVING

About 65 calories, 4 g fat (2 g saturated fat), 1 g protein, 15 mg sodium, 9 g carbohydrates, 0 g fiber

25 Days, 25 Ways to Decorate Sugar Cookies

Countdown to Christmas with festive cookies that are easy to pull off — whether you're starting with store-bought dough or making a homemade recipe (page 18).

Choco-Dipped Trees

Roll out dough and cut into trees using a cookie cutter. When cool, dip half of each tree into melted dark chocolate and sprinkle with multicolor nonpareils.

Sprinkle Mittens

Roll out dough and cut into mittens using a cookie cutter. When cool, decorate with icing, colored sprinkles and mini marshmallows.

Peppermint Drops

Roll dough into 1-inch balls; place on a baking sheet, spacing them 2 inches apart. Pat to flatten. After removing cookies from the oven, press a peppermint candy kiss into the center of each cookie.

Glazed "Waffle" Cookies

Roll out dough and cut into rounds using a cookie cutter. Gently press a potato masher into dough to form a pattern before baking. Tint icing with red food coloring and thin with water. When cookies cool, paint pattern with icing.

Holiday Snickerdoodles

Roll dough into 1-inch balls and then roll in a small bowl of cinnamon sugar; place on a baking sheet, spacing them 2 inches apart. Pat to flatten slightly.

Crunchy Candy Canes

Roll out dough and cut into candy canes using a cookie cutter. When cool, drizzle with melted white chocolate and sprinkle with crushed peppermints as desired.

White-Christmas Drops

Roll out dough and cut into rounds using a cookie cutter. When cool, spread with vanilla frosting. Sprinkle with edible silver leaf.

White Chocolate Sparklers

Roll out dough and cut into squares using a cookie cutter. When cool, dip diagonally into melted white chocolate and then sprinkle with green sanding sugar.

Stained-Glass Ornaments

Roll out dough and cut into ornaments using a cookie cutter. With a smaller cutter, cut out centers. With a straw, poke a hole in the top of each cookie for a ribbon. Bake for 7 minutes, then fill each hole with ¼ to ½ teaspoon crushed hard candies. Bake for another 3 to 5 minutes. After cookies cool, thread ribbon through holes.

Glazed Holly Hearts

Roll out dough and cut into hearts using a cookie cutter. When cool, outline and fill with red, green or white Royal or Decorator's Icing thinned slightly with water. Spoon icing in contrasting colors into a piping bag fitted with a small writing tip, then pipe on patterns.

Thumbprint Jammers

Roll dough into 1-inch balls and roll in a small bowl of mini nonpareils; place on a baking sheet, spacing them 2 inches apart. Make indentations in centers. When cool, fill centers with your favorite jam.

Swirly "Gumdrops"

Roll out dough and cut into candy shapes using a cookie cutter. When cool, decorate with icing.

Vanilla-Glazed Cookies

Roll dough into 1-inch balls; place onto a baking sheet. While cookies bake, whisk together 1 cup confectioners' sugar, 4 to 5 teaspoons milk and 1 teaspoon pure vanilla extract. Dip cooled cookies into glaze; sprinkle with nonpareils.

Sparkling Wreaths

Roll out dough and cut into wreaths using a cookie cutter. Tint icing with green food coloring. When cool, decorate cookies with green icing and then press into green sanding sugar. With a dab of icing, place 3 mini red M&M's onto each cookie.

Candy Cane Wands

Before dividing dough into disks, remove half from the mixing bowl. Beat in red food coloring and 1/2 teaspoon peppermint extract. Shape dough into 2-inch strands. Twist strands together, one of each color.

Glazed Stockings

Roll out dough and cut into stockings using a cookie cutter. When cool, decorate with icing and small nonpareils.

Classic Linzers

Roll out dough and cut into fluted rounds using a cookie cutter. With a smaller cutter, cut middles out of half the rounds. When cool, spread jam onto whole rounds. Dust cutouts with confectioners' sugar. Make sandwiches.

Santa's Boots

Roll out dough and cut into boots using a cookie cutter. When cool, outline with red icing, then decorate cuffs with white icing and top with white nonpareils.

Sprinkle "Donuts"

Roll out dough and cut into rounds using a cookie cutter. With a smaller cutter, cut middles out of rounds. When cool, spread with vanilla frosting and decorate with red, green and white sprinkles.

Candy Bells

Roll out dough and cut into bells using a cookie cutter. When cool, decorate with icing, matching sanding sugar and mini M&M's.

White Chocolate Trees

Roll out dough and cut into trees using a cookie cutter. When cool, drizzle with melted white chocolate and green candy melts.

Cranberry-Pistachio Wreaths

Roll out dough and cut into wreaths using a cookie cutter. When cool, decorate with white icing. Stud with finely chopped dried cranberries and pistachios.

Toasted Almond Slices

Roll out dough and cut into rounds using a cookie cutter. Before baking, press sliced almonds into dough to create a shingle pattern.

Granola Spice Wheels

Roll out dough to ¼ inch thick; cut into small rounds using a cookie cutter. Press 2 teaspoons granola into each round before baking.

Nutty Snowballs

Roll dough into 1-inch balls and then roll in a bowl of finely chopped pecans. Place onto a baking sheet, spacing them 2 inches apart. Pat to flatten. While warm, dust with confectioners' sugar. Let cool.

Recipe Index

Recipe Index

Recipe Index

Cover and book design by 10Ten Media
Library of Congress Cataloging-in-Publication Data is available.

10 9 8 7 6 5 4 3 2 1

Published by Hearst Home, an imprint of Hearst Home Books/Hearst Magazine Media, Inc.
300 West 57th Street, New York, NY 10019

Good Housekeeping, Hearst Home, the Hearst Home logo, and Hearst Home Books are
registered trademarks of Hearst Communications, Inc.

For information about custom editions, special sales, premium and
corporate purchases: hearst.com/magazines/hearst-books

Printed in United States of America
978-1-950785-88-9

PHOTO CREDITS

Mike Garten: Front Cover, 5, 7, 15, 19, 26, 27, 31, 37, 41, 43, 45, 47, 51, 57, 63, 65, 71, 83, 87, 88, 91, 93, 95, 99, 106, 112, 114, 123, 125, 129, 141, 147, 151, 153, 157, 159, 161, 179, 181, 183, 189, 191, 192, 195, 197, 199, 201, 203, 205, 207, 213, 217, 219, 223, 227, 229, 233, 242, 243, 244, 245, 246, 247; Alvaro Goveia: 6; Andrew Purcell: 69; Anjelika Gretskaia/Getty Images: 8, Back Cover; Aygun Ali/Shutterstock: C2, 1; baibaz/Getty Images: 11; Becky Luigart-Stayner: 103, 127, 239; Brian Woodcock: 58, 60, 121, 134, 148, 155, 169, 209, 221; Burcu Avsar: 29, 67, 81, 136, 171; burwellphotography/Getty Images: 34; Colin Faulkner: 139; Con Poulos: 77, 79, 143, 173, 174, 185, 193, 214, 231, 240; Diana Taliun/Getty Images: 13; DonNichols/Getty Images: 12; dulezidar/Getty Images: 2-3; Jeffrey Westbrook: 133; JGI/Jamie Grill/Getty Images: 16; jultud/Shutterstock: 13; Kat Teutsch: 75, 85, 165; Kate Mathis: 167, 105, 225, 244, 246; Marcus Nilsson: 73, 117, 237; margouillat photo/Shutterstock: 21; Marina Demidiuk/Getty Images: 22; Pamela Uyttendaele/Shutterstock: 26; pepifoto/Getty Images: 12; Philip Friedman/Studio D: 23; Ren Fuller: 49, 119, 163; Ryan Dausch: 55; Sarah Anne Ward: 32, 109, 131; Seregam/Shutterstock: 14; sockagphoto/Shutterstock: 242; Steve Giralt: 39, 52, 53, 97, 118, 235; stuartbur/Getty Images: 13; timquo/Shutterstock: 25; violetkaipa/Shutterstock: 13; Yunhee Kim: 145